Randle Wilbraham Falconer, Anthony Beaufort Brabazon

History of the Royal Bath Mineral Water Hospital

Randle Wilbraham Falconer, Anthony Beaufort Brabazon

History of the Royal Bath Mineral Water Hospital

ISBN/EAN: 9783743325050

Manufactured in Europe, USA, Canada, Australia, Japa

Cover: Foto ©ninafisch / pixelio.de

Manufactured and distributed by brebook publishing software (www.brebook.com)

Randle Wilbraham Falconer, Anthony Beaufort Brabazon

History of the Royal Bath Mineral Water Hospital

HISTORY

OF THE

ROYAL MINERAL WATER HOSPITAL

BATH,

BY

THE LATE RANDLE WILBRAHAM FALCONER, M.D.,

CONTINUED TO THE PRESENT TIME

BY

ANTHONY BEAUFORT BRABAZON, M.D.

"*Publica morborum requies, commune medentum
Auxilium, præsens numen, inemta salus.*"
Claud. Eidyl. 49 v. 69.

𝕿𝖍𝖎𝖗𝖉 𝕴𝖘𝖘𝖚𝖊.

BATH:
PRINTED FOR THE PRESIDENT AND GOVERNORS OF THE
ROYAL MINERAL WATER HOSPITAL, BATH, BY CHARLES HALLETT,
BLADUD BUILDINGS AND BRIDGE STREET.
1888.

Dedicated

TO THE

PRESIDENT, GOVERNORS, DONORS,

AND

SUBSCRIBERS,

ROYAL MINERAL WATER HOSPITAL,

BATH,

BY THEIR FAITHFUL SERVANT,

A. BEAUFORT BRABAZON, M.D.

August, 1888.

PREFACE.

THE whole of the edition of the admirably written History of the Royal Mineral Water Hospital, Bath, by the late Dr. Randle Wilbraham Falconer, being now exhausted, the President and Governors of the Institution have kindly entrusted to me the task of writing a Continuation of his work to the present time.

In doing so, to the best of my ability, I have followed the lines laid down by Dr. Falconer, by simply adding a fourth part to the three parts which constituted his work.

I need scarcely say I have not ventured to alter a line in the composition of a man so singularly gifted in felicity of expression, and who, at the same time, was so thoroughly acquainted with the subject as was my late colleague. I have, however, for the more ready reference of readers, placed the interesting and valuable notes at the foot of each page to which they apply, instead of at the end of the book, as in the former edition.

I have much pleasure in acknowledging the valuable assistance I have received from my friend, Mr. Peach, by whom the original work was published, in the editorial arrangements of the new edition, and in kindly revising the proofs as they issued from the press.

I must also thankfully acknowledge the assistance readily and kindly afforded to me by Mr. Dingle, the very efficient and intelligent Registrar of the Hospital.

A. BEAUFORT BRABAZON, M.D.

12 Darlington Street,
    Bath.

CONTENTS.

Chapter I.—From 1711 to 1841   9

,,   II.—From 1842 to 1861   62

,,   III.—From 1861 to 1863   84

,,   IV.—From 1864 to 1888   99

HISTORY

OF

THE GENERAL HOSPITAL,

NOW KNOWN AS

THE ROYAL MINERAL WATER HOSPITAL,

BATH.

Chapter I.

IN the year 1597, an Act of Parliament received the Royal assent, by which a right to the free use of the BATHS OF BATH was given to the diseased and impotent poor of England; and the sum of money which they were entitled to carry with them, to defray the cost of their journey, was limited, and they were also forbidden to beg on their way. Previously, however, to this date, Justices of the Peace, in the several counties, were empowered to license such persons to travel to the healing springs of BATH for the cure of their ailments.*

---

* "Such two Justices may * * * license diseased persons living of alms to trauell to Bathe or to Buckstone, for remedie of their griefe."—*The Office of the Justices of the Peace.* By *William Lambard*, 1588, 2nd edit., *p.* 334. "Anno tricesimo nono Regin. Eliz., cap. iv., A.D. 1597. An Act for Punishment of Rogues, Vagabonds, and sturdy Beggars."—"None resorting to Bath or Buxton to beg."

These acts caused the city to be inundated with beggars, of whom many, though ostensibly frequenting it for the use of the waters, were more intent upon the alms which fortune might grant them from the purses of the charitable and opulent who congregated at the springs, than upon anything else. Thus the mineral waters of Bath became a focus of attraction to beggars of various characters, insolent, vociferous, and sturdy, who were generalized, and are still commemorated, in the proverb, "*Beggars of Bath.*" *

In 1714, the Act above referred to was repealed, doubtless to the great satisfaction of the visitors and residents of the city; but the beggarly stream still continued to flow towards it, under the old pretext; and, in order effectually to check imposition, and with the view of relieving those who really were objects of compassion, the establishment of a

---

* "*Beggars of Bath.*"—"Many in that place; some natives there, others repairing thither from all parts of the land; the poor for alms; the pained for ease. Whither should fowl flock in a hard frost, but to the barn door? Here, all the two seasons, being the general confluence of gentry. Indeed, laws are daily made to restrain beggars, and daily broken by the connivance of those who make them; it being impossible, when the hungry belly barks and the bowels sound, to keep the tongue silent. And although oil of whip be the proper plaister for the cramp of laziness, yet some pity is due to impotent persons. In a word, seeing there is the Lazar's Bath in this city, I doubt not but many a good Lazarus, the true object of charity, may beg therein."—*Fuller's Worthies*, co. Somerset. "Such multitudes of Beggars come hither, partly for cure, and partly for relief, that the '*Sturdy beggars of Bath*' are become a proverb."—*Mackay's* Journey through England, Let. viii., *p.* 413, 1732. The expression "*Go to Bath*" not improbably arose from the circumstance narrated above; the importunate beggar of distant localities being summarily dismissed with this curt advice to join his fellows at "The Bath."

Chapter I.

Hospital for their reception was mooted. About two years after (*cir.* 1716), Lady ELIZABETH HASTINGS* and Mr. HENRY HOARE proposed the founding of a GENERAL HOSPITAL for the benefit of proper objects of relief; and Sir JOSEPH JEKYLL shortly after was interested in the proposal, and promoted the scheme to the utmost of his ability. Dr. OLIVER † and Mr. NASH—otherwise known as "*Beau Nash*"—were also among its early supporters. OLIVER GOLDSMITH, in his life of the latter, when alluding to his many beneficent actions, says:—"But of all the instances of Mr. NASH'S bounty, none does him more real honour than the pains he took in establishing an hospital at BATH, in which benefaction, however, Dr. OLIVER had a great share. This was one of those well-guided

---

* *Lady Elizabeth Hastings* was a person of some note. Her character is briefly drawn under the name of "Aspasia" in the *Tatler*, No. 53. She was an intimate friend of Archbishop Sharp and Robert Nelson. Her aunt by marriage, Lady Huntingdon, built the Chapel in the Vineyards, Bath, known as Lady Huntingdon's Chapel.

† It is well to state that there were two Doctors Oliver. The elder was at one time attached to the personal staff of William III., and was afterwards Physician to the Fleet, and later he was appointed Physician to the Royal Hospitals of Chatham and Greenwich. He died in Bath April 14th, 1716. Although he never practised in Bath, he wrote a Treatise on Fevers and the Bath Waters; also a Practical Dissertation on the Bath Waters.

The second Oliver is he who was connected with this institution, and who was the illegitimate son of the former. As a man he was istinguished by every manly virtue; as a philanthropist he rendered great services to the Hospital; as a physican of 40 years' standing in the city, he was never excelled in activity or in skill. Dr. Oliver, indeed, was distinguished as the "Famous Dr. Oliver." The biscuits called "Oliver Biscuits" were the invention of Dr. Oliver.

charities, dictated by reason and supported by prudence. By this institution the diseased poor might recover health, when incapable of receiving it in any other part of the kingdom. As the disorders of the poor, who could expect to find relief at BATH, were mostly chronical, the expense of maintaining them there was found more than their parishes thought proper to afford. They therefore chose to support them in a continual state of infirmity, by a small allowance at home, rather than be at the charge of an expensive cure. An hospital therefore, at BATH, it was thought, would be an asylum and a place of refuge to those disabled creatures, and would, at the same time, give the physician more thorough insight into the efficacy of the waters, from the regularity with which such patients would be obliged to take them. These inducements, therefore, influenced Dr. OLIVER and Mr. NASH to promote a subscription towards such a benefaction. The design was set on foot so early as the year 1711, but not completed till the year 1742.* It was not, however, until the autumn of 1723, that a subscription was opened for carrying the proposal into effect.

Among four collectors, who at the commencement undertook to obtain subscriptions, was Mr. NASH, of whose devotion to the establishment of the Hospital we shall have presently more to say. The list of subscriptions obtained by Mr. NASH and his colleagues amounted to £273 12s. 1d. On the 2nd of October, 1723, the first general meeting of subscribers was held, when the heads of a scheme

* The Life of Richard Nash, Esq., &c. Second edition, p. 116. London, 1763.

were submitted to their approval. It is stated that this scheme was prepared under the direction of several eminent persons of almost all denominations; and among those interested in it were the LORD PRESIDENTS OF ENGLAND AND SCOTLAND, THE MASTER OF THE ROLLS,* and other eminent lawyers, and also Sir RICHARD STEELE, the friend and coadjutor of ADDISON in the publication of the *Spectator*.

The general intent of this scheme was to make provision "for poor lepers, cripples, and other indigent persons resorting to Bath for cure, well recommended, and not otherwise provided for, and to discriminate real objects of charity from vagrants and other impostors, who crowd both the church and the town to the annoyance of the gentry resorting here; and who ought, by the care of the magistracy, to be expelled and punished." This annoyance appears to have continued for many years after, as, about the middle of the year 1742, some of the Hospital Committee were appointed to meet the Corporation " to consult of the proper methods

---

* Lord Presidents of England and Scotland—Lord Carleton—Henry Boyle, brother to the second Earl of Burlington—was Lord President of the Council in 1721, and retained that office until his decease in 1725. In Mr. William King's book of Subscribers to the Hospital, is the following entry:—"Lord President of Scotland, £2 2s. od."—*Wood's Description of Bath*, vol. 2, *p.* 276. From "Beatson's Political Index," it appears that there were Lord Presidents of the Privy Council of Scotland from 1625 to 1702. Probably the personage set down in the list as Lord President of Scotland, was the Lord President of the Court of Sessions; if so, this office was held by Duncan Forbes, of Culloden, in 1737, and by Robert Dundas, of Arniston, in 1748. Sir Joseph Jekyll was Master of the Rolls from 1717 until 1738, and Chief Lord Commissioner of the Great Seal in 1755.

to clear the town of vagrants." No report, however, is made of the decision arrived at by the conference.

According to the scheme brought under the consideration of the subscribers in 1723, as above mentioned, it was arranged that certain gentlemen should be named, who at a time to be appointed were, "First, to inspect and examine into the number and condition of the poor cripples and other indigent strangers, proper objects of this charity, *now here for cure*, distinguishing those that ought to remain here, from those that are judged to be incurable, or are recovered, and should return; in order to provide for the relief of the former, during their necessary stay, and immediate dismission of the latter, and furnishing them with something towards the necessary expense of their return. Also, secondly, to make an estimate of what the expense attending such dismission will amount unto. Thirdly, likewise what apartments will be proper to be taken for the reception of those intended to be supported and relieved by this benefaction; and what will be the rent thereof, and fitting up the same; and other incident expenses; and what number may be provided for; so that a greater number may not be received, than the fund for the time being will, upon a reasonable computation, maintain." Of the money by this time collected, it was decided that £250 should be invested, and the balance, £20 12s. 0d., together with a sum not exceeding a fifth part of what should be contributed before the next (second) General Meeting of Subscribers, should be employed as above directed. At this meeting it was reported that £19 9s. 8d. had been "applied for the use of the poor people *at that time in the city.*" No record is discoverable as to the continuance of this mode of relief, and, judging from the nature of subsequent proceedings, it appears to have been relinquished, and attention entirely given to procuring a suitable site for the erection of the HOSPITAL.

Among the gentlemen to whom the guardianship of the subscriptions collected up to Oct. 2, 1723, was intrusted, were Mr. NASH, Mr. HENRY HOARE, Dr. CHEYNE (who published a work on the Bath Waters in 1720, and whose life, by Dr. GREENHILL, is worthy of perusal); Dr. BAVE, who lived in the house which was afterwards converted into the Bath City Dispensary and Infirmary and now forms the older and back part of the Bath United Hospital, and will probably in a short time be pulled down to afford space for the improvement of that Institution*; and Dr. QUINTON, who wrote several works on the "Mineral Waters of Bath," one of which, printed in 1733, he dedicated to Mr. NASH.† On the 4th October, 1723, the scheme

---

* This has been carried out.

† The title of the treatise is, "A Treatise of Warm Bath Water, and of Cures lately at Bath, in Somersetshire, plainly proving that it is more probable to cure diseases by drinking Warm Mineral Waters and bathing in them, than in Cold Mineral Waters.—By John Quinton, M.D. Printed in the year MDCCXXXIII.," *pp.* 4 to 99. The dedication to Beau Nash is as follows:—"To that worthy and true Benefactor of the City of Bath; and Encourager of all the Diversions, and Pleasures there enjoy'd, so necessary to render the Medicinal Waters efficacious for the Recovery of Health, *Richard Nash, Esq.*, this Treatise of Baths, with all gratitude, for the many Favours he has conferr'd on me, is Humbly Dedicated by, Honour'd Sir, Your most Obedient, Oblig'd, Humble Servant, JOHN QUINTON."

having been fairly engrossed, was submitted to the subscribers for confirmation. Nothing took place in 1724 or 1725, except a single meeting, at which the Treasurer was appointed, and the vacancies in the Committee caused by deaths were filled up. There was no meeting held in 1726, and matters appeared to be in a languishing condition. In the early part, however, of 1727, Mr. Wood, the architect, pressed upon the Trustees the propriety of taking a portion of the ground at the north corner of the Ambrey,* then an open space, upon which St. James's Parade and the buildings adjoining the river, and in the direction of Milk Street, have since been erected. This suggestion was attended to, and designs made for a hospital; one was for a quadrangular, and the other for a circular building, each calculated for the reception of *sixty* patients, and in each, provisions was made for a bath. In Wood's ground-plan of Bath, dated 1735,† the number 30 refers to "an Hospital intended for 60 poor strangers." A small thick circular line marks the spot on the map which represents the locality above mentioned, and the same is repeated in maps of Bath, dated 1755, 1759, and 1760, many years after the present hospital was opened for the reception of patients.

In 1728, an order was made to treat with Mr. Gay (whose name is perpetuated in Gay St.), the owner of the property, for the land required. In 1730, at the general meeting of the Trustees, it was

---

* The name "Ambury" is still retained in a street connecting Corn Street with the Broad Quay on the river bank.

† The book containing the plan was not published until 1742.

stated that Mr. Gay was prepared to present them with the ground required, which generous offer was accepted; and, in consequence of considerable support being promised to the undertaking, the plans for the Hospital were greatly enlarged, and a design eventually completed for the accommodation of *one hundred and fifty* patients. It appears that the Trustees addressed a letter to Mr. Gay in reference to his proposed gift, which, however, met with no reply. He subsequently intimated that he would not part with more ground than would be sufficient for a building which would accommodate *sixty* patients. The designs were consequently again altered, and one, as approved by Mr. Gay, submitted to the Trustees, April 29, 1731, at Lindsey's Assembly House, which stood near the south-eastern end of the Abbey. The plan was engraved and printed and with it an address was published. The expense of building the hospital and furnishing it was estimated at £2,500. At this period of the proceedings, the necessary legal measures were taken for the conveyance of the land to the Trustees, during the progress of which, some person, represented as inimical to the building of the Hospital, obtained the remainder of the tenant's lease of the ground, amounting to a period of eight years, and the Trustees were, in consequence, compelled to seek for a new site, and several years elapsed before an eligible one presented itself.

On the 2nd Feb., 1737, Mr. BENJAMIN HOARE was appointed Banker in London to the charity, and the banking firm under this name have continued to be its London Bankers up to the present time, viz.: for a century and a half. In the same year Dr. OLIVER made an offer of some land for the erection of the proposed hospital, but though, at first, it was accepted, the decision was afterwards declared void without any recorded reason. In the same year an Act of Parliament was passed for the suppression of play-houses, and the theatre, together with two dwelling-houses, and some out-houses, near the *Upper Borough Walls*, or *St. Mary's Rampire*, and adjoining the *Bath Rectory House*, were offered to the Trustees for purchase, and accepted.

It may here be mentioned, that the first regularly-built theatre in Bath was erected in 1730,* and was the property of a widow, named *Poore*, and managed by *Hornby*, a comedian. It was afterwards purchased by LADY HAWLEY, the theatre being, as it is said, under her Ladyship's ball-room, and the seats reaching to within four feet of its floor; but subsequently it became the property of Mrs. CARNE,† or CAIRNE, and a Mr. DILLON also had some interest in the property.

From the period of the purchase of this site, after "*surprising disappointments*," as the Hospital records state, matters appear to have progressed favourably. The Trustees issued an address to the public soliciting their support, which was printed in the newspapers.

On the 9th of February, 1738, Mr. Wood pro-

---

* Wood, in his Description of Bath, refers to a theatre erected at an earlier date, namely, in 1705, vol. II., pp. 288 and 445.

† The family of Carne was descended from Sir Edward Carne, who was Queen Elizabeth's ambassador to Pope Julius III. During his embassy he gave some curious information to Andrias Baccius, who gave the substance of it in his book—"*De Thermis*"—a book now worth its weight in bank notes.

duced perfected designs for the Hospital to be erected on the site of the theatre, and also a fair plan and elevation of the same, which being approved by the Trustees, Mr. NASH was requested to take them to London for the purpose of submitting them to the inspection of HIS MAJESTY and the ROYAL FAMILY, after which they were conveyed to Mr. PINE, to be engraved. A copy of this design, together with the address to the public,* framed,

---

* This design is printed at the head of a large sheet, and below it, a plan of the hospital, having on the west side Vicarage Lane, and the garden attached to the Bath Rectory House, on the site of which the new portion of the Hospital is erected; on the east, is the "Bear Inn" yard. In front, "St. Mary's Rampire, now called the Bur Walls, over which there is an open view of the country from the Hospital." The address to the public is headed, "The plan and Elevation of a new General Hospital intended to be erected at Bath for the reception of one hundred and fifty poor strangers. Anno Dom. 1737." In the tympanum is delineated a design from the parable of the Good Samaritan, and under the pediment is inscribed, "*Go and do thou likewise.*" As this address is rarely to be met with, it is here given:—" The usefulness of hospitals for the reception of sick people, is so well known, that it is needless to say anything of it. The frequent and noble benefactions to St. Thomas's and St. Bartholomew's, in London, &c., shew the conviction people have, after long experience, that such donations are true charity. It is upon this general principle of relieving the poor and distressed, that many well-disposed persons have set on foot, and hope to establish, an Hospital at Bath. And what more particularly moved them to promote this work was, the consideration that in many cases the diseased poor might there recover their healths, which they could not do from any other charity, or by any other means whatsoever. The care of the physician, the assistance of the surgeon, and the medicines of the apothecary, may be had in any other part of the kingdom; but the benefit of the Bath Waters, in their full virtue, can only be enjoy'd at the fountain-head. The expense, indeed, of living at Bath long enough to receive a cure, is greater than most parishes are able or willing to defray; and therefore they chuse rather to support their poor cripples, by a small allowance at home, than be at the charge of

and glazed, is hung in the *Registrar's Office*, at the *General Hospital*. The principal front, as represented in the engraving of the Hospital, corresponds with the elevation of the old building, with the two

endeavouring their relief by maintaining them at Bath. Few parishes are free from such persons, who, by the loss of their limbs, are become a burden to themselves and their neighbours, and drag on an uneasy life, which, by God's blessing on the charity here proposed, might be render'd comfortable to themselves, and profitable to the public. It would be endless to enumerate the many different cases in which the like good effects of this Charity might reasonably be expected; and surely, a consciousness of having been the instruments, under GOD, of the restoration of such objects from misery to ease, from impotence to strength, and from beggary and want, to a capacity of getting an honest livelihood and comfortable subsistence, would be so sincere a pleasure to all good minds, that they must think it cheaply purchased by a generous contribution towards so good a work. But, though the relief of our miserable fellow-creatures might be sufficient to induce all good-natured persons to promote this charity, especially those who have themselves felt the benefit of these healing Waters; yet it may not be amiss to mention another very great advantage that will accrue to the publick from such an Hospital being founded at Bath. All physicians allow, that the greatest certainty that can be attained to in the knowledge of the nature and virtues of any medicine, arises out of the number of observations of the effect it has on human bodies in different circumstances. The world is indeed greatly indebted already to many worthy and learned gentlemen of the faculty, who have published their observations on the Bath Waters, and given the histories of their patients' cases with great exactness. These histories are very valuable, and greatly assist the present practitioners in the performance of the many cures which numberless living witnesses can now testify that they have received upon the place; but, surely, if the knowledge of the nature and efficacy of these Waters could still be render'd more extensive and certain, it would be doing great service to every individual person, who may hereafter, in any country or age, have occasion for their use. Nobody can doubt but that this Hospital will greatly contribute towards this desirable end, who considers, that persons of higher rank, are too often negligent of their own health; and, by no means, so exact in taking their medicines, abstaining from things which hurt them, and staying a due time, as could be wish'd, and is indeed necessary, in order to give the

following exceptions, namely: an additional story has been erected, which was built in 1796, and from the tympanum over the entrance, has been omitted the design taken from the Parable of the

Physician a sufficient opportunity either of doing them all the service their case would admit of, or of making observations for the future benefit of others. Whereas, in this Hospital every person will be under his government and direction in all circumstances regarding his health; so that a few years will furnish more histories of cases which may be depended upon (if the Physicians keep due registers of the sick under their care) than any man's private practice could have done in an age. And it is to be hoped, that the success which may reasonably be expected from the regularity of these poor creatures, may induce others of better condition voluntarily to imitate them in the management of themselves, that they may receive the like benefits. Everybody may therefore see how great an advantage this Hospital will be to the public. The sick will be healed, many parishes eased of the burden of their useless poor cripples, and the knowledge and use of the Bath Waters will be greatly improv'd to the benefit of all succeeding generations. It being necessary, for the promoting, carrying on this charity that persons of honour and reputation should take it into their protection and guardianship; the contributors present, have agreed, 'That every person contributing twenty pounds, or any sum exceeding that, towards this charity, shall be admitted a Governor of this Hospital. It is proposed by the contributors present, to build an Hospital capable of receiving and commodiously entertaining one hundred and fifty poor, distressed persons. The expence of building the said Hospital, according to the above draught, and of furnishing the same with beds, and other necessaries, it is thought, upon the most moderate computation, will amount to the sum of Six Thousand Pounds. Any persons inclin'd to encourage this undertaking, are desir'd to send their contributions to RICHARD NASH, Esq.; FRANCIS FAUQUIER, Esq.; and Dr. OLIVER, at Bath; or Mr. BENJAMIN HOARE, Banker, at the Golden Bottle, in Fleet Street, London; or leave their subscriptions with them for the use of this charity; and they may be assur'd, that all such donations shall be faithfully applied to the purposes intended by the donors, and a monthly account published by Mr. HOARE, of all such donations. Effectually to prevent any poor persons coming to Bath, and being burdensome to the town, under a pretence of desiring to be admitted

Good Samaritan. This design was never completed, although an order was given to *Mr. Mathyssens* to cut it in freestone, and that he "*be paid the sum of twenty-five guineas for the same*"; a model, also, was subsequently made, for which, and several

into the said Hospital, the following order for such admission is agreed on, *viz.*—The person proposed shall first have his case drawn up by some Physician or skilful person in his neighbourhood, which, being duly attested by the Minister and Churchwardens of the Parish he resided in, and transmitted to the Physicians of the said Hospital, together with the age of such person, shall by them be carefully considered and examined; and if they find that the person is a proper object of this charity, they shall signify such their judgment to the Minister of the said Parish; and so soon as there is a vacancy in the said Hospital, shall notify it to him by letter, for the person to come within a limited time, who is to bring back these letters of the Physicians to the Minister; by which he or she is to be admitted into the said Hospital; and if any person shall come to Bath, under pretence of proposing himself to the Hospital, contrary to this order, he shall not only be refused admittance, but be treated as a vagrant, with the utmost severity of the law. Every Parish sending a person to the Hospital, shall supply him with thirty shillings, which, upon his admission, shall be lodged in the hands of the Treasurer of the Hospital, to defray the charge of his funeral, in case he dies in the Hospital; or to be returned to him whenever he is discharged from thence, to answer the expense of his journey to his own abode. Whenever any person is proposed to the Physicians of the Hospital, and is adjudged by them to be a proper object, he shall be immediately minuted down to succeed to the next vacancy that shall happen; and every person so minuted, shall absolutely succeed in his turn, any interest or application from any person whatsoever notwithstanding. These articles are all that are now thought necessary to be settled by the contributors present; but as soon as the foundation of the Hospital is laid (publick Notice whereof will be given in some of the Papers), General Meetings of the Trustees and Contributors will be appointed, for them to consider and settle such farther regulations as they shall then judge to be for the good of this charity. These articles are submitted to the judgment of the publick: and all persons are desired to give their opinions as to any alterations or additions, to promote the good which is intended by all the contributors."

drawings of the same, he was paid five guineas. In reference to the engraved plan, Mr. WOOD says:— "the printed plan of the HOSPITAL was for the sake of ornament, and, to gain a point in the purchase of the land, made different from that which was intended for execution; but when the last bargain was completed for a stable belonging to Mr. WILLIAM BOYES, at the south-west corner of the land purchased of Mrs. CARNE or CAIRNE, I produced the real plan to the Trustees, who, approving of it, 25th August, 1738, ordered it to be carried into execution instead of that which was printed." The resolution confirming this change is as follows:— "Resolved, that the wards of the Hospital be enlarged, and other alterations from the plan as permitted to be made according to a new plan brought this day by Mr. WOOD, the Physicians apprehending that large wards will be more conducive to the health of the Patients." Wood's statement and the resolution will explain the cause of the difference between the actual arrangements of the ground-plan of the present HOSPITAL, and the plan which had been engraved.

On the 24th April of this year, the subscriptions amounted to £2082, and, on the same day, the workmen commenced pulling down the old outbuildings. Mrs. ANNE CAIRNE was paid £630 for the play-house, on the 9th May; on the 25th, directions were given to pull down the theatre, and on the 30th its destruction was commenced. When the rubbish had been cleared away, and sufficient space made, the foundation stone was laid on the 6th July, at the north-eastern corner of the intended building, that ceremony being performed by the Right

Hon. WILLIAM PULTENEY, afterwards EARL of BATH. The following inscription was cut upon the foundation stone :—" *This stone is the first which was laid in the foundation of the* GENERAL HOSPITAL, *July the sixth, A.D.* 1738. GOD PROSPER THIS CHARITABLE UNDERTAKING." A memorandum appears in the records of the Hospital of the date of the laying of the foundation stone, and of the inscription placed on it; no mention, however, is made of the individual by whom it was laid.

On the 15th January, 1738, the accounts of the Treasurers, Dr. WILLIAM OLIVER, RICHARD NASH, Esq., and FRANCIS FAUQUIER, Esq., were examined and approved, " from the 2nd of March, 1737, being the commencement of this charity." But the sums collected in 1723, " to be employed as well towards the immediate relief of poor strangers then in Bath, as towards a fund for building an Hospital for such poor necessitous persons, as being not otherwise provided for, that come to this place for the use and benefit of the Bath Waters," are included in the report published on the 15th January, 1738. The commencement of the charity, so far as regards the raising of funds for the erection of a Hospital, is incorrectly stated in the report to have been on the 2nd March, 1737.

In February of the same year, it appears from the following resolution that arrangements were made with the MAYOR and CORPORATION of BATH, for the use of the *Mineral Waters* by the Hospital patients :—" Resolved, that the offer of the CORPORATION to the *Trustees* of the new HOSPITAL, by Councillor Roberts, be accepted, and the thanks of the *Trustees* be returned to the CORPORATION for their said offer of the free use of the HOT BATH, and the old Pump, for the use of the sick persons belonging to the said HOSPITAL."

On the 19th April, 1739, the subscriptions amounted to £4,268; and in this year an act of Incorporation was obtained, the ruling body being recognized under the style and title of the PRESIDENT and GOVERNORS of the HOSPITAL or INFIRMARY at BATH.* THOMAS CAREW was appointed first PRESIDENT, at a *General Meeting of Subscribers*, held July 16th, 1739, and on the 24th he appointed Dr. OLIVER, *Deputy-President*, who, with Dr. E. HARINGTON† and Dr. A. RAYNER,

---

* This Act was intituled, "An Act for Establishing and well governing an Hospital or Infirmary in the City of Bath," and was passed in the 12th year of the reign of George the Second. An Act was subsequently passed in 1779, by which the President and Governors of the Hospital were more effectually enabled "to take or acquire, and hold, any Lands, Tenements, or Hereditaments, and any Money or Personal Property, to be laid out in Lands, &c., pursuant to any Will, or otherwise, to the amount limited in the said Act." This Act restricted the Corporation to holding landed property, the income from which exceeded one thousand pounds yearly. A third Act was passed in 1830, by which alterations were made in the first Act, but which enabled the Corporation to effect a most important improvement, namely, the formation of Baths *in* the Hospital, and the conveyance, with the consent of the Mayor and Corporation of Bath, of the Mineral Waters from the King's Bath Spring to the Hospital Baths.

† *Dr. E. Harington.*—I have not succeeded in identifying this gentleman, but he is thought to have been a member of the distinguished family of the same name. He resigned the office of Physician to the Hospital in 1750. [This Dr. Harington, whom Dr. Falconer was not able to identify, was the 6th son of John Harington, Esq., J.P., co. Somerset, by his marriage with Helena, eldest daughter of Benjamin Gostlett, Esq., of Marshfield, co. Gloucester. He was born at Kelston, 1696. Entered Wadham College, Oxon, 1712. B.A., 1715. M.A., 1718. Bach. Med., 1722. Med. Doc., 1726. Buried at Kelston, 8th August, 1757.]

were appointed *Physicians* to the HOSPITAL, on May 1st, 1740, and Mr. J. PEIRCE,* *Surgeon.* Mr. CAREW continued in the office of PRESIDENT until 1741, when he was succeeded by the Hon. LIEUT.-GENERAL WADE.† The first meeting of the PRESIDENT and GOVERNORS of the HOSPITAL, under their Act of Incorporation, was held at Mr. Cogswell's Rummer Tavern, Cheap Street, and several previous meetings were held at the same place ; but it was not until Monday, Jan. 19, 1741, that the Governors first met in the new building, when rules for the management of the charity were agreed to ; an annual subscription was opened in November for the maintenance of the patients ; and, on Christmas Eve,‡ the first matron, Mrs. Whitlock,

* This was Jerry Peirce, who was the intimate friend of Dr. Oliver. Peirce was of the family, if not directly descended from Dr. Peirce, of the Abbey House, where he received Queen Anne on one occasion, and to whom he was physician. Jerry Peirce lived in a curious little house, called Lilliput Castle, built by Wood, on the site now called "Battle Fields." The picture of Oliver and Peirce examining a patient, painted by Hoare, hangs in the board-room. Oliver and Peirce resigned on the same day—May 1, 1761. Oliver died in 1764, and was buried in the Abbey.

† *General Wade.*—In the Guildhall are preserved a few of the remaining portraits of Members of the Bath Corporation, "painted by *Van Dyce* at the expense of General Wade, as a compliment for their free and unanimous choice of him as their representative in three successive Parliaments. His is also in the Hall."—*Vide* " The Stranger's Assistant and Guide to Bath," *p.* 54, 1773 ; said to have been written by Dr. William Falconer, M.D., F.R.S. One of the lost portraits, that of Ralph Allen, was recovered by W. Bush, Esq., when Mayor of Bath, in 1856. General Wade was returned Member for Bath, in 1722, 1727, 1734, and 1741. The Rev. F. Kilvert was preparing at the time of his decease, in 1863, a biographical sketch of General Wade, but died before he was able to complete it.

‡ The Meetings of the Committee were, at this period, generally held late in the afternoon or in the evening.

was appointed. Immediately after this meeting, it is stated by Wood that a benefaction of £2,000 was paid to the Treasurer by Mrs. JANE HOLDEN; it appears, however, on reference to the Hospital minutes, that this legacy was received from Mrs. JANE HOLDEN as executrix of her late husband, SAMUEL HOLDEN, Esq. On Tuesday, May 18th, 1742, the institution was opened for the reception of patients.

One of the principal features of this charity was, that poor persons were admitted to it, "*from any part of Great Britain or Ireland*," and no inhabitant of the city of Bath was allowed admission. This regulation, WOOD states, was affirmed at a meeting of the Trustees on March 23rd, 1737. But no such limitation was then made. The resolution passed at that meeting was as follows:—" It is proposed by the contributors present to build an Hospital capable of receiving and commodiously entertaining one hundred and fifty poor distressed persons, from any part of Great Britain or Ireland." But in November, 1743, the following resolution was passed, viz., " That the inhabitants of this city are excluded admission into this Hospital by Act of Parliament." This exclusion, however, only affected those who resided within the limited area of the city walls. This resolution, however, was rescinded in 1835;* but, notwithstanding, it is now open to those who were excluded; the number annually admitted is very small, as in 1855, out of five hundred and three

---

* This question originated a considerable discussion among the Governors, and the admirable and exhaustive view taken of the subject at the time by the Rev. Dr. Falconer, M.D., though it failed to secure a majority opposed to the rescinding of the resolution, has been since regarded as a true and just exposition of the view entertained by the founders of the Hospital.

patients admitted, only ten were from the old Bath parishes, and, as the facilities for affording the poor of the city access to the public baths have of late years been much increased by the Corporation, even the small number who now apply for admission into the Hospital will probably be diminished. In 1779, a second Act was passed to enable the Corporation "to take or acquire, and hold, any Lands, Tenements, or Hereditaments, or any interest in Lands, Tenements, or Hereditaments, and any Money or Personal Property, to be laid out in Lands, Tenements, or Hereditaments, pursuant to any Will, or otherwise, to the amount limited in the said Act. In 1830, a new Act was obtained by the Governors of the Hospital, by which they were enabled to construct baths on the Hospital premises, and lay down pipes in the public streets for the conveyance to them of the hot mineral water, which was, according to an agreement, supplied by the Corporation of the city, and for other purposes. By this arrangement the patients, who had previously to be carried to the bath in quaint-looking machines, or sedan chairs, as they were called, of curious construction, were enabled to bathe at a short distance from their wards; and a staff of chairmen, supported at the expense of the charity, whose conduct is represented as being extremely obnoxious and irregular, was dissolved.*

The Hospital records commenced on Feb. 23rd, 1737, the most prominent entry of which day's proceedings is the following, signed by Mr. Allen:—

---

* On one occasion it appears that some of the chairmen and patients were found intoxicated at the Hot Bath, the former procuring the spirits for the purpose.

Chapter I.

"*I do hereby promise and oblige myself, my executors, and administrators, to deliver, at my wharf, in the Dolemead, adjoining the city, free of all expenses, all wrought free stones, paving stones, wall stones and lime, which may, from time to time, be wanted to build and complete the new General Hospital intended to be erected in this city on the ground lately purchased of Mrs. Cairne, commonly called the Old Playhouse, to such person or persons as the Treasurer of the said Hospital for the time being shall appoint to receive the same.*

"RALPH ALLEN.*

"Witnessed by James Sparrow, Francis Fauquier, W. Oliver."

Independently of this donation, Mr. ALLEN, on several occasions, gave in different sums to the charity, £1,600, which included £500 for furnishing the Hospital, and £400 when its funds were so diminished as to necessitate the reduction of the number of patients to forty, and also a bequest of £150 from POPE, devised by the latter in the following terms:—
"*In case* R. ALLEN, Esq., *above said, shall survive*

---

* In 1857, the late Rev. F. Kilvert published a very interesting sketch of "Ralph Allen and Prior Park," which contains, it is believed, all the information respecting Mr. Allen which can, or at least could then, be obtained of him. There is also a short notice of this gentleman in the supplement (*p.* 13) to Monkland's "Literature and Literati of Bath," published in 1855. There are several portraits of Mr. Allen. In the 5th edition of Bishop Hurd's "Moral and Political Dialogues," published in 1776, which are dedicated to the memory of Mr. Allen, there is a masterly and spirited medallion of him, etched by W. Hoare, bearing date 1764. There are two marble busts of Mr. Allen: one in the Entrance-Hall of the Hospital, and another in the Council-Room of the Guildhall.

me, I order my executors to pay him the sum of £150, being, to the best of my calculation, the amount of what I have received from him, partly for my own, and partly for charitable uses. If he refuse to take this himself, I desire him to employ it in a way I am persuaded he will not dislike—to the benefit of the BATH HOSPITAL." The following entry in the Hospital Minute Book occurs May 7, 1755:—"*A benefaction of* RALPH ALLEN, *Esq., which was a legacy of the late* ALEXANDER POPE, *Esq.,* £150." *
Mr. ALLEN was elected a member of the Committee in 1728, and President of the Hospital in May, 1742, and was one of the Treasurers for many years. The bust, in the vestibule of the Hospital, of this noble supporter of the charity, was the gift of Dr. Warburton, Bishop of Gloucester, who married Mrs. Allen's niece (Gertrude Tucker), to the President and Governors, by whom it was thus acknowledged:—"*The Governors of the General Hospital, met in Committee, April 27th,* 1757, *return their thanks to the Reverend Dr. Warburton, for his kind intention of making a present of a bust of Ralph Allen, Esq., to the Hospital—a present most acceptable, as it will perpetuate a more lively remembrance of that great benefactor to this charity, and to which it will remain an honour to have had so worthy a promoter, longer than marble will endure.*"

The same records bear ample testimony to the perseverance of Mr. NASH in aiding the establishment of this charity; and there are but few pages of its transactions which do not contain proofs of the regularity of his attendance at the meetings of

---

* See Pope's Will, printed at the end of the 9th volume of his works, edited by Warburton.

the Trustees, and of the interest which he uniformly manifested in its welfare. He was appointed one of the Treasurers of the Hospital in 1738, and held that office until his decease in 1761. His first donation to the charity, as stated in the report of 1738, was £100, and in the space of about six years, a sum of more than £2,100 was paid by him to the Treasurer of the Hospital, consisting of donations obtained by his individual exertions. His biographer, OLIVER GOLDSMITH, relates the following anecdote relative to his soliciting support for the Hospital:—
"The sums he gave and collected for the Hospital were great, and his manner of doing it was no less admirable. I am told that he was once collecting money in Wiltshire's Room for that purpose, when a lady entered, who is more remarkable for her wit than her charity, and, not being able to pass him unobserved, she gave him a pat with her fan, and said 'You must put down a trifle for me, Nash, I have no money in my pocket.' 'Yes, Madam,' says he, 'that I will with pleasure, if your Grace will tell me when to stop;' then taking a handful of guineas out of his pocket, he began to tell them into his white hat, one, two, three, four, five. 'Hold, hold,' says the Duchess,* 'consider what you are about.' 'Consider your rank and fortune, Madame,' says Nash, and continued telling six, seven, eight, nine, ten. Here the Duchess stormed, and caught hold of his hand. 'Peace, Madam,' says Nash, 'you

* The lady was the Duchess of Queensbery. She was the daughter of Henry, Earl of Clarendon and Rochester. It has been said by some writers that it was the Duchess of Marlborough, but that is erroneous. The flippancy displayed was very characteristic of the former lady, who was the wife of "Old Q.," as the Duke was commonly called.

shall have your name written in letters of gold, Madam, and upon the front of the building, Madam;' sixteen, seventeen, eighteen, nineteen, twenty. 'I won't pay a farthing more,' says the Duchess. 'Charity hides a multitude of sins,' replied Nash; twenty-one, twenty-two, twenty-three, twenty-four, twenty-five. 'Nash,' says she, 'I protest you frighten me out of my wits; I shall die!' 'Madam, you will never die with doing good; and if you do, it will be the better for you,' answered Nash, and was about to proceed, but perceiving her Grace had lost all patience, a parley ensued, when he, after much altercation, agreed to stop his hand, and compound with her Grace for thirty guineas. The Duchess, however, seemed displeased the whole evening; and when he came to the table where she was playing, bid him 'stand farther, an ugly devil, for she hated the sight of him.' But her Grace, afterwards having a run of good luck, called Nash to her. 'Come,' says she, 'I will be friends with you, though you are a fool, and to let you see I am not angry, there is ten guineas more for your charity. But this I insist on, that neither my name, nor the sum, shall be mentioned.'"* A casual visitor to Bath says:— "I cannot quit Mr. NASH without observing, to his honour, that he is no less a promoter of public charity than a hero in every diversion. You see him as complaisant and diligent with the basin at the Abbey, to collect alms for the hospital and charity children, as he is busy in getting subscriptions for balls. His memory, perhaps, will be revered and loved for the good accruing from the General Hospital, which he zealously forwards, and hath already brought to some

* The Life of Richard Nash. Second Edition : *p.* 121, Lond., 1765.

perfection, long after his foibles and his favour hath ceased to be the ambition of the young and the gay."*

In reflecting on the numerous acts of levity which attach to the name of BEAU NASH, the recollection of his earnest advocacy of the interests of the General Hospital ought to have its due weight, and should soften the asperity of the critic who would represent him as wholly occupied in folly and frivolity. In the Pump Room there is a marble statue of Nash, by PRINCE HOARE; the right hand of the figure rests on a pedestal, having on the face of it an open scroll, on which is delineated a plan of the General Hospital; there is also an admirable crayon portrait of Nash, in the possession of the Corporation, presented to that body by Captain B. PEACH, the Treasurer for the City and Borough of Bath, and another in oils, in the Mayor's room at the Guildhall; there is also a smaller portrait in crayons, in the Board-room of the General Hospital.†

Having mentioned the munificent gifts of the benevolent ALLEN, and the unwearied exertions of NASH, in support of the Hospital, the generous conduct of WOOD, the architect, cannot pass unnoticed. The following memorandum, signed by WOOD, who was elected a Governor of the Hospital in October, 1739, occurs in the Hospital records:—

"*I, John Wood, of the city of Bath, architect, do hereby give all the several draughts, plans, and other papers relating to the Hospital at Bath, together with my care, labour, and expenses for surveying and direct-*

---

* Gentleman's Mag., *p.* 345; 1745.

† This portrait bears date 1742, the year in which the Hospital was first opened for the admission of Patients.

ing the building of the said Hospital, as a free gift and benefaction to the said Hospital; and I do hereby accordingly acquit and for ever discharge the Corporation of the said Hospital, from all debts, dues, or demands, whatsoever. Witness my hand this first day of *March*, 1741.—*Jo. Wood*."*

Mr. WOOD was frequently appointed on Sub-Committees where important matters were to be considered, and continued an active member of the Court of Assistants or Committee, until his decease in 1754. In 1766 Mr. WOOD's son presented a Cup and Salver for the Communion Services at the Hospital.

In 1740 an Act was passed to amend an Act for the more effectual preventing of excessive and deceitful gaming, by a clause, in which it was provided that a moiety of the fines incurred under it, in the county of Somerset, should "go and be applied to, and for the use and benefit of the poor persons admitted into the Hospital or Infirmary lately erected in the city of Bath, for the benefit of poor persons resorting to the said city, for the benefit of the Mineral Waters there."†

---

* *John Wood.*—This gentleman was the architect of many of the finest buildings of Bath. He was also the author of a Description of Bath, which has conveyed to the present time an amount of information regarding its condition and progress afforded by no other author previous to his time. He died May 23rd, 1754, leaving a son, who inherited his father's architectural taste, and added buildings remarkable for their beauty, to Bath.

† The Act is intituled, "An Act to restrain and prevent the excessive increase of Horse Races, and for amending an Act made in the last session of parliament, intituled, 'An Act for the more effectual preventing of excessive and deceitful gaming.'" The clause referred to is as follows :—"§ vi.—And be it further enacted by the authority aforesaid, that all penalties and forfeitures incurred by

The year 1741 was employed by the Governors principally in making arrangements for furnishing the house, for supplying it with provisions, and generally providing for the reception of patients. Preparatory to opening the Hospital, Regulations were drawn up by Dr. OLIVER as to the admission and removal of patients, which after receiving the approval of the Governors, were printed, and a large number distributed throughout the kingdom, many being sent to places of known public resort in London.

On the 18th May, 1742, the Hospital was opened for the reception of patients. Three physicians— namely, Dr. W. OLIVER, Dr. E. HARINGTON, and Dr. A. RAYNER—and one surgeon, Mr. JEREMIAH PEIRCE,* had been elected in 1740; and in June, 1742, four other surgeons—namely, Mr. A. CLELAND, Mr. T. PALMER, Mr. H. WRIGHT, and Mr. J. DONNE—were appointed. These gentlemen formed the first medical board of the charity. In the autumn of this year,

---

any person or persons for any offence against this act shall be sued for and recovered by any action, bill, plaint, or information in any of his Majesty's Courts of Record at Westminster, or at the Assizes, and shall be disposed of, one moiety thereof to the use of such person or persons as shall so sue for the same, and the other moiety to the use of the poor of such parish or place where the offence shall be committed ; except such one moiety of such penalties or forfeitures as shall be incurred by, and recovered of, any person or persons within the county of Somerset; which said one moiety shall go and be applied to and for the use and benefit of the poor persons admitted into the Hospital or Infirmary lately erected in the city of Bath, for the benefit of poor persons resorting to the said city for the benefit of the Mineral Waters there."—An. decim. tert. George II. cap. xix., Stat. at Large., vol. vi., p. 397.

* *Mr. Jeremiah Peirce.*—There is a bust of this gentleman in the Hospital. He resigned his office of surgeon to the charity in 1761.

the funds of the Charity being in a languishing condition, several gentlemen, among whom was Dr. DAVID HARTLEY,* were requested to go from house to house to solicit annual subscriptions.

The most prominent event of the following year was the dismissal by the Governors of Mr.' A. CLELAND from his office of Surgeon to the Hospital, which took place on the 21st September, on account of misconduct. This event was the source of much warm discussion among the public, and several pamphlets were printed on the occasion. A narrative of the whole proceedings was published by the Governors of the Hospital.†

The financial position of the charity does not appear to have been materially improved by the efforts made in 1742, for in 1744 it was found necessary to reduce the number of patients to forty. On this occasion Mr. MORRIS, the House Apothecary, offered, with singular generosity, to reduce his salary from sixty to forty pounds a year; and with a view to render the charity less dependent on the fluctuating sources of voluntary support, it was resolved, "That all single benefactions of fifty pounds or upwards be

---

* Dr. David Hartley was elected one of the physicians of the Hospital, May the 15th, 1744, and resigned that office November 2nd, 1748. He died in 1757, at Hartley House, Belvedere. His son was member for Hull, and was one of the early promoters of the abolition of the slave trade.—Monkland's Literature and Literati of Bath, *p.* 11, and Supplement, *pp.* 79 and 81.

† This statement was in reality published "by the Governors of the Hospital who voted for Mr. Cleland's Dismission." It is entitled "A short vindication of the proceedings of the Governors of the General Hospital at Bath in relation to Mr. Archibald Cleland, &c.; to which is prefixed a short Narrative of the Proceedings," 8vo, *pp.* 34. 1744.

applied towards raising a perpetual fund for the support of the Hospital, unless otherwise specified by the donor." Subsequently to the passing of this resolution, Mr. FRANCIS COLSTON gave one hundred pounds a year for three years, on condition that the number of patients should be increased to forty-five. The offer was at once accepted, and the condition which accompanied it agreed to.

On the 1st May, 1744, Mr. FRANCIS COLSTON was elected President of the Hospital. No notice of his resignation or decease occurs in the minutes, but on the 29th January, 1745, it was resolved, at a General Court of Governors, "That the Treasurers of this Hospital apply to H.R.H. the PRINCE OF WALES, humbly desiring his acceptance of the Presidentship of this Hospital." On the 26th February, the following entries occur in the minutes:—" At this General Court his Royal Highness FREDERICK, PRINCE OF WALES, was unanimously elected President of this Infirmary." "Ordered, that Mr. NASH be desired to return the thanks of this Court to His Royal Highness for the honour and favour he does them in accepting to be their President." On the 1st May, 1746, H.R.H. was re-elected; he was again re-elected on the 1st May, 1747, and also on the 1st May, 1748; but on the 18th of this month Mr. NASH produced a letter to the Court of Governors "from SIR WILLIAM IRBY, acquainting him that H.R.H. is unwilling to act longer as President of this Hospital." On the same day the Hon. B. BATHURST, Treasurer of the Hospital, reported "that he had received a benefaction of one hundred pounds, by Mr. NASH, from H.R.H. the PRINCE OF WALES." On the 25th of May a General Court was held, and His Grace the DUKE OF BEAUFORT elected President in the room of the PRINCE OF WALES.

Early in 1747, the Governors having previously made a liberal regulation in favour of the admission of soldiers to the benefits of the charity—a large donation was made to the Hospital, under circumstances set forth in the following statement:—"*Received of* SIR RICHARD HOARE*, *the sum of one thousand pounds for the use of the* GENERAL HOSPITAL AT BATH, *being the benefaction to the said* HOSPITAL *by the subscribers to the subscription carried on at the Guildhall (London) towards the relief, support, and encouragement of the soldiers employed in suppressing the late Rebellion, in consideration of the readiness shewn by the Governors of the said Hospital in relieving maimed and wounded soldiers, and to the intent that they may continue the like charitable benevolence to them for the future.*" The thanks of the Governors for this munificent gift were ordered to be conveyed by Dr. OLIVER to H.R.H. the PRINCE OF WALES, H.R.H. the DUKE OF CUMBERLAND, and Sir RICHARD HOARE, and the rest of the subscribers "*for their several good offices towards this Hospital in procuring one thousand pounds to the capital fund.*"

In 1749, HENRY Lord COLERAINE, Baron of Coleraine, in the Kingdom of Ireland, executed a deed of gift by which the sum of five hundred pounds was given for the support and maintenance of one patient, over and above the number of patients who might be admitted into the Hospital, to be

---

* Sir Richard Hoare, Knt., was Lord Mayor of London in the memorable year of the Scottish Rebellion, 1745. His son, Henry, by his second marriage, married Mary, daughter of William Hoare, Esq., R.A., of Bath. The large picture in the Board Room of the General Hospital, representing Dr. Oliver and Mr. Peirce attending on patients, and also an Altar-piece at the Octagon Chapel, were painted by this artist. He died in 1792.

called Lord COLERAINE'S patient. In June, 1762, the above sum was invested in the Old South Sea Annuities, and there has been ever since a patient in the Hospital benefiting by this gift. A legacy also of two thousand pounds was received this year from the family of WILLIAM CURZON, Esq., which, according to the tenor of the bequest, was to be laid out in land.

In 1750, the expenses of the Hospital much exceeded the receipts, and it was found necessary again to reduce the number of patients admitted to it from one hundred and twelve to eighty, and although in the following year the full number of patients was admitted, it was reduced to ninety in 1757, and in 1758 further reduced to seventy; in 1765 it was augmented to one hundred and five, and in 1769 to one hundred and twelve, and in 1783 the number was reduced to ninety, there being nearly £600 due to the Treasurers; but by the 21st of May, in consequence of numerous donations and subscriptions, the debt was paid off, and the resolution for diminishing the number of patients was rescinded; shortly after which the number was increased to one hundred and thirty-four.

The Charmy Down Estate was purchased by the Governors for the charity, on the 1st June, 1750, under powers granted by the Act of Incorporation.

By the first Act of Parliament passed for the government of the Hospital, it is directed that previous to the admission of a patient a sum of money—now called "Caution-money"—should be deposited with the Treasurer. The amount for a patient, coming from any part of England or Wales, is fixed at Three Pounds, and from Scotland or Ireland at Five Pounds. These sums are demanded in order to defray the cost of removing to their homes the patients when discharged from the Hospital. In 1756, Dr. OLIVER drew up, at the request of the Governors, the regulations for the admission of Scotch and Irish patients, which are given at length in the Hospital minutes.

In 1758 when the funds of the charity were diminished and the number of patients reduced, an oratorio at the Abbey took place for the benefit of the Hospital, and as it proved successful—the sum obtained amounting to £161 14s. 1d.—it was determined that there should be a similar performance every spring and autumn. The subsequent oratorios however, were not so successful as the first, and they appear to have been relinquished, by common consent, after 1759.

The following minute occurs in the proceedings of the Hospital Committee, under date 1st April, 1761. "DANIEL DANVERS, Esq., one of the Treasurers, acknowledges to have received a note of hand of one hundred pounds of RICHARD NASH'S, Esq., deceased, payable to RALPH ALLEN, Esq., which note RALPH ALLEN, Esq., gives as a benefaction to this Hospital, and DANIEL DANVERS, Esq., promises to account for the dividend the said note shall produce to the Hospital.—Resolved that the thanks of the Committee be returned to RALPH ALLEN, Esq., for his benefaction of Mr. NASH'S promissory note to the Hospital." From subsequent minutes, it appears that during 1762, the year after NASH died, £42 8s. 9d. was paid on account of his note of hand.

In 1762, the thanks of the General Court were ordered "to be sent to Mr. WILLIAM HOARE, for the elegant picture he has presented to this Hospital." The subject of the picture is not mentioned, but it is probably that of Hygeia, which is in the present board-room of the Hospital.

In 1767 a small burial ground outside the portion of the Upper Borough Walls, opposite to the new portion of the Hospital, was conseccrated. As early as 1743 an attempt was made to provide a burial ground for the Charity, but legal technicalities interfered to prevent its acquisition ; eventually, however, the Corporation arranged that the fee simple of the ground should be vested in the President and Governors of the Hospital, and its consecration was thus secured. This burial ground was closed in June, 1849, and a tablet attached to the western wall bearing an inscription, nearly the whole of which is now illegible.*

For some time the duties of Chaplain to the inmates of the Hospital were discharged gratuitously, but in 1770 the necessity for appointing a Chaplain with a fixed salary was brought before the Governors. At this time it was thought undesirable to make use of the ordinary funds of the Hospital for remunerating a Chaplain for his services, and consequently it was proposed to raise a sufficient sum by subscription for that special object, and, in addition to what might thus be obtained, it was determined that £15 should be taken from the amount of Church collections for

---

* By the kindness of J. H. Markland, Esq., D.C.L., I am enabled to give the inscription, which was as follows :—" This piece of ground was in the year 1736 set apart for the burial of Patients, dying in the Bath General Hospital, and, after receiving 238 Bodies, was closed by the Governors of that Charity in the year 1849 from regard to the health of the living." A text was added, but it is doubtful whether it was taken from the Revelation of St. John, chap. xi., vv. 25, 26, or from 1 Cor., chap. xv., vv. 42, 43, 44. [It is well to state that the ground is bounded on the south by a fragment of the ancient wall. This wall, which was much dilapidated, was repaired and the battlements restored to their original condition.—*Editor of new edition.*]

the Hospital, until such time as a fund should be established for providing a suitable salary for the Chaplain. In 1775 the amount directed to be paid for this purpose from the subscriptions was £30 a year; the surplus, if any, was to be retained by the Treasurer, and set apart towards forming a fund from which the Chaplain's salary might be paid; to this fund the sum of £100 was contributed by the Hon. JOHN JEFFERYS PRATT,* in 1782. In 1831 it was resolved that £33 12s. should be paid to the Chaplain out of the Hospital funds, and in 1844 his salary was fixed at £120 a year, which sum was, and is now, paid out of the general income of the Hospital. In the Hospital minutes of 1856, the following entry occurs:—" A fund for payment of a Chaplain, the produce of subscriptions raised in 1776 and subsequent years, and invested in the names of the Treasurers of the Hospital as Trustees, £600, reduced 3 per cents. The dividends paid to the Chaplain, with an addition from the funds of the charity, until the stock was transferred into the name of the President and Governors by Mr. JOHNSON PHILLOTT, the executor of the last surviving Trustee, Mr. CHARLES PHILLOTT, in 1842; an act, passed in 1830, having previously given power to the Governors to pay the stipend of a Chaplain out of the funds of the Hospital."

On the 5th November, 1778, a Committee was appointed "to consider of what application may be necessary to be made to Parliament for relief under the present statute of Mortmain." On the 18th of the same month, it was "resolved that the representatives of this City—viz., Sir J. SAUNDERS SEBRIGHT, Bart.,

---

* The representative of Bath in Parliament and afterwards Marquis Camden.

and ABEL MOYSEY, Esq.—be requested to move Parliament for the relief of this Hospital, in order to accelerate their obtaining the value of one thousand pounds per annum, and that it be referred to the committee already appointed for this purpose to settle the method and for carrying this application into execution." The committee reported, Dec. 1st, that it was found necessary, after taking the opinion of the Attorney General, to apply to Parliament to accomplish the object in view, and forwarded a request to the Mayor, that his assistance and that of the Corporation generally might be afforded them "in the matter intended to be petitioned for." The Corporation having passed a resolution "to instruct and desire the representatives of this city to support the petition of this Hospital," and the same being reported to the Committee, a draft petition was read and approved, and communication opened with the Recorder of the city, and its representatives, as well as with members of the House of Lords and Commons, whom it was thought might be disposed to give their support to the petition. Mr. DANIEL DANVERS was appointed by the Committee to attend in London, and full power given him to do what was requisite to promote the progress of the Bill through the Houses of Parliament. It was read a third time, and passed the House of Commons on March 10th, 1779. On the 12th March it was read a second time in the House of Lords, and shortly after received the Royal assent. Mr. DANVERS on his return to Bath, stated that W. BROMLEY CHESTER, Esq., Sir Ed. BAYNTUN, Bart., PAUL METHUEN, Esq., CHARLES BARROW, Esq., and ED. PHELIPS, Esq., "were particularly active in their support of the petition to Parliament," and therefore they were recommended to the Court to be elected Governors of the Hospital.

In 1780, Dec. 13, the thanks of the Board were given "to WILLIAM HOARE, Esq., for his valuable present to this Hospital of the picture of the late DANIEL DANVERS, Esq. And that he be requested to make this Hospital a present of his own." A deputation was appointed to wait on Mr. HOARE for this purpose. The portraits of Mr. DANVERS and Mr. W. HOARE are suspended in the present board room of the Hospital.

In 1782 it was ordered "that thanks be returned for the recovery of patients in this Hospital, on the last Sunday in every month, at all the places of Divine Worship in this city." For how long this order continued in force, or whether it was superseded by an order made in 1786, does not appear.

In 1785 Mr. CHRISTOPHER ANSTEY composed those lines which were for many years placed in the principal Pump Room of Bath, and are still to be seen in its western vestibule. From the following resolution, which is in the minutes of the Hospital, these lines appear to have been written at the request of the Governors:—" Resolved, that the thanks of this Committee be returned to CHRISTOPHER ANSTEY in the following terms and signed by the Chairman (CHAS. PHILLOTT, Esq.), in behalf of the Committee: —'Sir, The Committee of the Governors of the General Hospital at Bath have directed me in the name of the whole body to return you their most grateful thanks for the very just and elegant manner in which you have fulfilled their wishes of informing the public in general of the real state of the Hospital.'" "Resolved, that a copy of Mr. ANSTEY'S inscription relative to this Hospital be handsomely printed and kept hanging from time to time in the several Pump Rooms." "Resolved, that a thousand copies of the above inscription be printed, and five sent to each Governor and two to each Subscriber."

The following paragraph from the *Bath Chronicle* of May 18, 1797, in reference to Anstey's lines, is as applicable at the present day as it was sixty-six years since :—

"It is the duty of all those who owe their health, the use of their limbs, their very existence, to the healing fountains of Bath, to think of their suffering fellow-creatures, pining in misery and affliction, whom the General Hospital was built to receive, and to administer the best advice and every other comfort their wretched situation demands. *Every parish in this kingdom ought to subscribe liberally to this excellent foundation;* it is for the accommodation of *their* poor it was built, and the doors are never shut to any poor creature whose case is adapted to the Bath Waters, and no recommendation of a subscriber or benefactor is here necessary. The following beautiful lines, written in the year 1783* (by ANSTEY, author of 'The New Bath Guide'), and then painted on the pump in the New Pump Room, cannot be too often impressed on the memories and consciences of the rich and good, who drink of these healing springs and bathe in the pool of Bethesda :—

> 'Oh! pause awhile, whoe'er thou art
> That drink'st this healing stream,
> If e'er compassion o'er thy heart,
> Diffused its heavenly beam :—
>
> Think on the wretch whose distant lot
> This friendly aid denies;
> Think how in some poor lonely cot
> He unregarded lies!

* 1785

> Hither the helpless stranger bring,
>   Relieve his heartfelt woe;
> And let thy bounty, like this spring,
>   In genial currents flow.
>
> So may thy years from grief and pain,
>   And pining want be free;
> And thou from Heaven that mercy gain
>   The poor receive from thee.'"

Mr. ANSTEY was a Governor of the Hospital and a member of the Committee, at the meetings of which he was a regular attendant, He died in 1805 at the house of his son-in-law, H. BOSANQUET, Esq., of Hardenhuish, near Chippenham, in his 81st year. His remains are interred in the parish church of Walcot, and a monument has been raised to his memory in Westminster Abbey.*

In 1786 the order was first given for the form in which patients "who shall find benefit in this Hospital" should return thanks through the ministers of the Churches or Chapels they may attend at their own homes. The form is to the present time regularly

---

* A very excellent portrait of Anstey has recently been bequeathed by the late Captain Montagu Montagu to the Corporation of Bath, together with an autograph receipt of Anstey's, to the following effect :—

"July 31, 1766.
"Received of Mr. Dodsley, the sum of two hundred and fifty pounds in full for the sole Right of the Copy of the New Bath Guide.
    Witness my hand, CHR. ANSTEY."

The following inscription on a mural tablet to the memory of Anstey is placed on the northern wall of Walcot Church :—

"In the vaults beneath are deposited the remains of CHRISTOPHER ANSTEY, Esq., born 31st of October, 1724; died 3rd August, 1805. A monument is erected to his memory in Westminster Abbey. In the same vault, William and William Thomas, sixth and seventh sons, and Sarah, his fourth daughter, late wife of — Sotheby, also the wife of Christopher Anstey. Nat. 7 May, 1732. Ob. 1 Jan., 1812."

The monument to his memory, in Poet's Corner, in Westminster

delivered to such patients, when discharged, at the weekly meetings of the Committee.

Abbey, was erected by his eldest son, the Rev. Christopher Anstey, inscribed with the following epitaph :—
"M. S.
CHRISTOPHORI ANSTEY arm :
Alumni Etonensis,
Et Collegii Regalis apud-Cantabrigienses olim Socii,
Poetæ
literis elegantioribus adprime ornati,
et inter principes Pœtarum,
qui in eodem genere floruerunt,
Sedem eximiam tenentis.
Ille annum circiter
MDCCLXX.
Rus suum in agro Cantabrigiensi
mutavit Bathonia,
quem locum ei præter omnes dudum arrisisse
testis est, celeberrimum illud Pœma,
Titulo inde ducto insignitum :
ibi deinceps sex et triginta annos commoratus,
obit A.D. MDCCCV.
et ætatis suæ
Octogesimo primo.

At non Pœtæ fama cum ipso peribit, quem legunt omnes, omnes quem requirunt, cujus carmine nullum in aures dulcius descendit melos, nullum memoria citius retinet aut lubentius. Proprium illi fuit materiem sui carminis, non nisi ex ipsa fontium origine haurire. Aliena vitavit tangere, aut si qua tetigit, pulchriora fecit, et sua. Perpaucis unquam contigit, aut in vita et moribus hominum posse acutius cernere, aut eorum leviora vitia, ineptias, pravæ Religionis deliramenta, et quicquid ficti sit, et simulati felicius adumbrare : Perpaucis ludere tam amabiliter : neque enim Ille Ridiculum suum insuavi vel acerbo miscebat, aut sales suos imbuebat veneno : delectare natus, non lædere. Pectus Illi tenerrimum fuit, Christiana benevolentai incoctum : Jocari autem, ac ludere versatili ejus ingenio non erat satis, potuit enim ad rem seriam ac lugubrem aliquando transcurrere, haud solertior lectori risum movere, quam tristi querimonia elicere lacrymas.

Hæc inter animi oblectamenta, Ille per vitæ semitam nec spe nec metu impeditam progressus, annos prius attigit seniles, quam senectutem sibi obrepentem senserat, ingenio adhuc vigens, cum memoria adhuc rerum tenaci, intus domique felix, honoratus foris, suavitate morum ac sermonum omnibus quibus consuevit jucundus, eorum autem quibuscum conjunctissime viverat, ipsis in præcordiis collocatus."—*The Poetical Works of the late Ch. Anstey, Esq., with some Account of his Life, etc.*, 1808, 4to, *p. lx.*

In the same year the thanks of the General Court of Governors was forwarded to the Medical and Surgical officers of the Hospital " for the trouble they had taken in collecting and arranging materials for publishing the effects of Bath Water on the Patients of this Hospital in Paralytic Cases," and directions were given that they should be printed at the expense and for the benefit of the Hospital, and be advertised as such. These cases were published in 1787, under the title of "Narrative of the Efficacy of the Bath Waters in various kinds of Paralytic Disorders, admitted into the Bath Hospital from the end of 1775 to the end of 1785, with particular relations of Fifty-two of their Cases."* This work was dedicated by the Physicians and Surgeons of the Hospital to the President, Lord VERNON, and other Governors of the Hospital.

In 1788 two benefactions were made to the Hospital funds, deserving of notice: one of an hundred and fifty pounds from T. BOWDLER, Esq., the produce of the sale of the copyright of his letters, written in Holland in the year 1787 ; the other, £20, from Miss H. M. BOWDLER, being a further part of the profits arising from the sale of the late Miss BOWDLER'S "Poems and Essays, printed for the benefit of the Hospital."† The profits of this publication were at

* Several of these cases are deserving of attention. They were taken from the Hospital Records of Cases, and arranged for publication, it is believed, by William Falconer, M.D., F.R.S., who was for five and thirty years Physician to the Hospital, and the author of several works of acknowledged merit on the Bath Waters, and other medical, as well as literary subjects.

† "As the profits arising from the sale of these poems and essays were applied to the benefit of the General Hospital at Bath, the writer's benevolent efforts seem to have been doubly useful, contributing at once to relieve the bodies and instruct the minds of her fellow

intervals given to the Hospital by Miss H. M. BOWD-
LER; on the 25th Aug., 1802, when the last sum
appears to have been paid, they amounted altogether
to £600. An edition of this work was published in
the Cabinet Library, 1824.

In 1791, the Governors of the Hospital appointed
a Committee "to inquire into the expediency of building a new Hospital," and the subject was also submitted
to the consideration of the Medical Board of the Charity,
who reported strongly and unanimously against its
removal. The Governors having decided against the
erection of a new Hospital, took into their consideration
plans offered by Mr. BALDWIN, who was the architect
of the Town Hall, the Pump Room, and adjoining
Baths, for enlarging and improving the present building. The subject, however, of the removal of the
Hospital was again revived and discussed at great
length, until January, 1793, when another architect,
Mr. PALMER, proposed a plan for adding a new story
over the front of the present hospital, which was
agreed to, and the contract for erecting it was sealed
on the 6th March following. An account of the discussions which arose on the proposal to remove the
Hospital between 1791 and 1792, is given in a
pamphlet entitled, "An Address to the Governors of
the Bath Hospital on the propriety of extending the
benefits of that humane and laudable Institution, by
several of the Governors, 1792." During the period
which was occupied by protracted discussions, an

creatures. After the approving testimony of so distinguished a
character as William Melmoth, Esq., and the sanction of the public
by the rapid circulation of numerous and large editions, it can scarcely
be necessary to add anything commendatory."—Preface to the Cabinet
Edition, *p.* viii.—*See Monkland's Literature and Literati of Bath, p. 42, and Bath and Cheltenham Gazette,* March 7, 1855, for notices of Miss Bowdler's family.

attempt had been made, but without success, for the accommodation of applicants, who were numerous, for admission to the charity. In 1795, the two new wards constructed by Mr. PALMER were named "Nash's" and "Colston's" Wards, the former of which was in this year completed for the reception of patients. In the same year also the Hospital became possessed of shares in the Assembly Rooms by the death of Lord ROKEBY, Primate of all Ireland, who bequeathed them to the charity for the support of two patients, who are to this time known as the Primate of Ireland's patients.

On the 1st May, 1806, the question of erecting a new Hospital was once more revived, and a portion of ground available for the purpose, in the neighbourhood of the Hot Bath, was reported on, and its capabilities considered. It seems, however, that on this occasion the subject was allowed to drop by common consent, as no final decision regarding it is recorded.

At the close of 1808, the following entry appears in the Hospital minute book of that year, to which recent events have given a more than ordinary interest:—" Major THOMAS FITZGERALD, one of the Executors under the last will of General JOSEPH SMITH, who bequeathed Five Hundred Pounds to the Hospitals in Bath, issuing out of a debt due to the testator by the NABOB OF ARCOT, having applied for the concurrence of the Governors of this hospital jointly with the other legatees to receive the said legacy in proportionable parts, as the said debt shall be paid, ordered that the same be acceded to." It is somewhat remarkable that this legacy had been overlooked by the representatives of the different charities to which it was bequeathed up to September 13th, 1859, when some information regarding it was incidentally given to FREDERICK DOWDING, Esq., who in consequence proceeded to make the necessary enquiries, and by consent of the representatives of the General Hospital, the United Hospital, and Bellott's Hospital, ultimately caused a petition to be presented to the Court of Chancery, in order to obtain the sums due to those Institutions. From a report on this subject, presented by Mr. DOWDING to the Municipal Charity Trustees, it appears that on the 20th April, 1790, JOSEPH SMITH, Esquire, formerly a Brigadier-General in the service of the East India Company, made his will of this date, and thereby bequeathed numerous legacies, and amongst them he gave " five hundred pounds to the different Hospitals at Bath, to the relief of such objects as are annually sent to them." The testator died on the 1st Sept., 1790, at Bath, and was buried in the churchyard at Weston, near that city, and his will shortly after proved by his Executors. On the 22nd Feb., 1814, a suit was instituted for the management of the testator's affairs, and by an order of the same date it was directed that the interest on the legacies should be computed at the rate of four per cent. per annum from the 15th of May, 1804; and that sum which was due to the hospitals of Bath should be paid into the bank with the privity of the Accountant-General of the Court of Chancery, to be placed to the credit of the cause, subject to the further order of the Court. From this time, until Sept., 1859, the interest had accumulated, and also the dividends from the sum invested in the funds. No investment was made after the year 1831. The Court of Chancery complied with the terms of the petition, and the sum ultimately paid to each of the Hospitals, after the expenses were deducted, amounted to £652 7s. 9d. stock, and £403 0s. 7d. in cash: total, £1,055 8s. 4d.

A tomb and monument, erected by the widow of General SMITH, at Weston, were in 1860 repaired and restored at the expense of the authorities of the three hospitals who benefited by the above legacy—viz., the President and Governors of the Bath General or Mineral Water Hospital; the Municipal Charity Trustees, as managers of Bellott's Hospital; and by the Trustees and Committee of the Bath United Hospital.*

Among the donations made to the Hospital in 1810 was the sum of £50 4s. 10d., being the profits arising from the sale of a Poem, called "The Months,"†

---

* On a monument to the memory of General Smith, in the parish church at Weston, near Bath, is the following inscription:—
"Sacred to the Memory of
BRIGADIER-GENERAL JOSEPH SMITH.
In early life he entered the military service of the East India Company at Madras; and by making the duty of a soldier his study and employment, he added to distinguished bravery professional knowledge; when advanced to the supreme Command, his conduct was altogether worthy of the trust reposed, while every military accomplishment established his reputation in public; the social virtues were amply displayed in his private retirement. Universal charity was the habitual practice of his life; and hope well-founded his support at the approach of Death. He departed this life at Bath, on the 1st of September, 1790, in the 57th year of his age." This monument, in addition to one erected over the General's remains in the adjacent Churchyard, was placed here by his disconsolate widow.

On the monument in the churchyard is this inscription:—
" Here is deposited the noblest work of God: an honest man, a brave officer, a loving and affectionate husband, a generous and most sincere friend,
GENERAL JOSEPH SMITH,
Who departed this life, September 1, 1790, aged 57. Regretted by all."

† There is a little history attached to this book. The author, to begin with, was a direct descendant from Peter Sherston, son of William Sherston, Mayor of Bath in Queen Elizabeth's reign. The book is a small quarto, beautifully printed on paper made at Combe Down Mills. It was bound in Bath, and was therefore in all respects a Bath book. There is a frontispiece and other illustrations, engraved after originals by T. Barker. The work was published by subscription, the price of each copy was half-a-guinea. Barker died in 1847, and is buried in Weston Churchyard.

by PETER SHERSTON, Esq., who resided at Stoberry, near Wells. The work was published in 1809, for the benefit of the General Hospital.

In the same year, namely, in 1810, the Committee of the Bath City Infirmary and Dispensary having communicated to the Governors of the Hospital a resolution not to claim any legacy unless bequeathed specifically to the Bath City Infirmary or Dispensary, it was ordered that the said resolution be filed with the papers of this Hospital.

In 1818, a proposal was made to add another ward to the Hospital at the Eastern or Union Street side of the building, as the number of invalids waiting for admission was forty-two. This proposal, however, was not adopted, inasmuch as it was considered that the erection of a ward in the situation contemplated would obstruct the access of light, and preclude the free ventilation of the building.

In 1824, the following minute appears in the proceedings of the Committee :—" The bequest of Mr. RICHARD JONES, of Dursley, in the County of Gloucester, in his will, bearing date 31st day of May, 1811, giving the sum of £250, three per cent. stock, to the Governors of this Hospital on condition that two out-patients and one in-patient should be annually admitted into this Hospital, which was acceded to ; but as there are no out-patients, it was proposed that the three patients should be all admitted as in-patients, and that the Treasurer do execute an undertaking in writing, in conformity to the said will to that effect ;" which was done in the early part of the year 1825, "on behalf of the Governors, to be delivered to the executors of the late Mr. JONES, who had acceded to the proposal that the three patients should be all received as in-patients." Patients coming from Dursley under the above provision, and not exceeding the number mentioned, are admitted into the Hospital without prepayment of "caution money."

In 1826, the payment of STRODE'S annual gift for poor lepers, coming to the Leper's Bath at Bath, together with arrears, was directed by the Court of Chancery, upon an application made by the President and Governors, founded on a report of the Commissioners appointed to inquire into Public Charities, to be then and subsequently paid into the funds of the General Hospital, as the objects intended to be relieved by this gift are now provided for by that charity. This gift was made by ELIZABETH STRODE, of Downside, in the county of Somerset, by will, dated March 20, 1712. The sum annually received by the Hospital on account of this bequest amounts to Five Pounds.

On the 1st of May, 1826, at a General Court, "CHARLES PHILLOTT, Esq., reported from the executors of the late Dr. PERRY that the following sums in the public funds, £26,064 4s. 1d. 3 per cent. Consols, and £3,216 6s. 3d. in the new 4 per cents., are now become the property of this Hospital, but as annuities are still to be paid amounting to £90 per annum, the executors propose keeping the latter sum in their hands to pay the same, handing over the surplus of the dividends to the Treasurer of the Hospital."

On June the 21st, 1826, application was made to the President and Governors of the Hospital on behalf of Mr. THOS. PERRY'S sisters and niece for them to receive the proceeds of the stock up to the time of Mr. PERRY'S decease, namely, in March of this year. The estate was not considered by the applicant liable to pay the Annuities of this year, as they were not due until the May succeeding Mr. THOMAS PERRY'S decease, Dr. PERRY having died in May, 1825. In reply to this application, the President and Governors considered that both questions raised in the application should be decided by the Executors of the will of the late Dr. WILLIAM PERRY, as they could not undertake to decide legal points or "dispose of any property belonging to the Hospital otherwise than for the benefit of the Patients."

On the 26th July, 1826, at a General Court, "Mr. TUGWELL, one of the executors of the will of the late Dr. WILLIAM PERRY, having attended this meeting and having proposed that in consequence of the death of the late THOMAS PERRY, Esq., the legatee for life of the residue of the property (subject to certain annuities charged thereon), the stock now constituting such residuum, after deducting the legacy duty and other necessary charges—should be transferred into the names of the President and Governors of this Hospital, that the annuities now due should be paid out of the dividends received in the present month, and that such annuties should in future be paid by the Hospital instead of the executor." This proposal was acquiesced in by the Governors, and their thanks given to Mr. TUGWELL for his attention to the interests of the Hospital on this occasion. In memory of Dr. WILLIAM PERRY'S munificent bequest, one of the new wards in the older portion of the Hospital building has been recently named "PERRY'S WARD."

Until the year 1827, two sermons had been annually preached in the Churches and Chapels of Bath, one in April and another in December, for the benefit of the Hospital. From this time the December sermon only was preached. Upon what grounds this alteration was made does not distinctly appear, as upon this point the minutes are imperfect. It seems, however, that some remonstrance was made upon the subject by the Archdeacon of Bath and the Rector of Walcot. The following extract from reasons given against the charge by one of the Governors who dissented from it, affords almost the only clue to the discussion which followed the proposed alteration: "Because it seemed more prudent to maintain a diminished number of patients *for one year* upon the remainder of the revenue of the Hospital, permanent and contingent, unaided by collections of contributions at the several Churches and Chapels of this city, in order to leave to the Dispensary and United Hospital the undivided benefit which might be derived from such collections, and at the expiration of that period of one year to report to the public, what number of patients the Governors were actually enabled to admit, and whether the late accession of property accruing from the bequest of the late DR. PERRY had superseded all future appeals to their liberality."

The change, however, was effected, and only one sermon is now annually preached at the churches and chapels for the benefit of the Hospital. During recent years, the proceeds from these sermons have materially diminished in amount.

At the latter part of 1828, it was decided that the whole Hospital should undergo a complete examination, preparatory to its entire repair, and it was ordered that on and after the 1st of January, 1829, no more patients should be admitted than could be received into the wards which were not being repaired. On this occasion arrangements were made for introducing warm air into the wards, and also gas—in the earlier days of the Charity the wards were lighted by means of lanterns—and for the ventilation of the Hospital generally. Greatly, however, as these improvements contributed to the comfort of the patients, the most

Chapter I.

important change, in many respects, was the erection of Baths in the Hospital for the use of the Waters by the patients, and thus rendering it unnecessary for them to be carried to the Hot Bath for the purpose of Bathing. The introduction of the Mineral Water into the Hospital was due to a suggestion made by the then Resident Apothecary, Mr. BUSH, who received the cordial thanks of the President and Governors for his proposal.

The repairs of the Hospital were completed about the middle of 1829. The Baths, however, were not completed until the 25th Jan., 1831, when they were for the first time used by the Patients, as it was necessary not only to obtain the consent of the Corporation to draw the water from their springs, but also to obtain an Act of Parliament for powers to introduce the Mineral Water into the Hospital, and to lay down pipes for its conveyance through the public thoroughfares from the King's Bath Spring to the Hospital, which Act did not receive the Royal assent until the 2nd June, 1830.

On the 29th of December, 1827, at a Special General Court, a letter, dated 14th Nov., 1827, was read from Messrs. COUTTS and Co., Bankers, London, stating that, by the decease of Lieut.-Col. FREDERICK SACKVILLE, late of the Bengal Army, who died at Richmond, Surrey, on the 18th of October, 1827, the sum of £100 had been left to the Hospital, and £50 to twelve widows, residing in Bath, of known respectability, and each having a family of not fewer than three children, and labouring under sickness, misfortune, and poverty. These widows were to be selected by the Governors of the Hospital, within the space of twelve months after the decease of the testator, and in the event of the Governors of the Hospital not making the selection within the time directed, then it was to be made by the Society of Noblemen and Gentlemen instituted in Bath for the Relief of Poverty in Distress. The letter from Messrs. COUTTS stated, that the testator had left property in England and also in India, and that as the former did not quite suffice for the discharge of the bequests made under the will, it would be necessary to obtain information as to the Indian property before they were paid. It was not until the 11th of December, 1828, that Messrs. COUTTS were able to state that they were in a position to pay the legacies bequeathed by Col. SACKVILLE'S will; consequently the period had elapsed during which the Hospital Governors were empowered to select the twelve widows. As, however, the power had been lost by circumstances over which the Governors had no control, they were still desirous of making the selection, but as the terms of the will were imperative, it was ultimately arranged, that considering the peculiar features of the case, a statement should be made to the Society upon whom the selection devolved, and that a request for joint action in the matter should be made, which was agreed to, and on the 2nd of February, 1829, arrangements were completed by the Governors appointed by the Hospital and the Society for the Relief of Poverty in Distress, for the selection of the recipients of Colonel SACKVILLE'S bounty.

On the 17th of October, 1829, Mr. W. B. FARNELL died; who had been for nearly forty-four years House Apothecary to the Hospital. In consequence of his increasing infirmities—he was eighty years of age when he died—and in consideration of the faithful and assiduous manner in which he had performed the duties of his office, the Governors, in February, 1828, had appointed an assistant to him. In October of the following year, being incapable of any longer discharging his duties, a successor was appointed, and at the same time a resolution was passed, that Mr. FARNELL be "maintained and lodged in the house at the expense of the Institution, and that every possible attention which can contribute to his personal comfort be paid him." Not long after this resolution was passed, Mr. FARNELL died, and the Committee being desirous of giving further expression to their appreciation of his character and regard for his memory, requested the attendance of the members of their body at his funeral, which took place on the 23rd of October, 1829, at the Abbey. Near the place of his interment was erected a tablet to his memory by a friend, and his portrait is in the Hospital Board-room. Mr. FARNELL left by will a legacy of two hundred pounds to the Hospital.*

During the period when the draft for the new Act of Parliament for obtaining a supply of Mineral Water to the baths in the Hospital and for other purposes, was under the consideration of the Governors, a question arose as to the legality of the admission into

---

* "On Monday, a neat tablet was placed in the Abbey Church to the memory of Mr. Farnell, late apothecary to the Bath General Hospital, bearing the following inscription :—

'Near this place lie the remains of W. B. Farnell, Apothecary for nearly forty-four years to the General Hospital in this City. He died Oct. 17, 1829, aged 80 years. His faults are before his Maker; man must remember his good deeds. He was a benefactor to the Hospital by bequest, and more so by his virtues and example. The grateful, when they see his name, will speak of him and praise God. Stranger, as thou can'st, lessen the evils of life. This memorial is placed here by a Friend, who may thus cherish gratitude in others, and is bound to testify his own.' "—*Bath Chronicle*, Dec. 16, 1829.

the Hospital of persons residing in Bath. This question was referred to counsel, whose opinion was in favour of their admission, consequently a clause was inserted into the draft of the act declaratory of such right. The Bill, as amended in the Committee and in the House of Commons, was read at a special General Court and approved, and the corporate seal affixed to it on the 17th of May, 1830.

This question, however, was revived on the 2nd of May, 1831, when it was moved that the opinions of the Attorney and Solicitor-General, should be taken upon the construction of the Act as to the right of the poor of the City of Bath to be admitted to this Hospital. An amendment was proposed to this motion :—That the original intention of this Hospital, as expressed in the preamble of the Act of Parliament, excluding the inhabitants of the City of Bath, be acted on." The amendment was carried, eleven voting in favour of it, and nine against it. But on the 1st of May, 1835, " It was resolved that the resolution which was passed on the 16th of November, 1743, which declared the Inhabitants of Bath to be excluded from admission to the Hospital, be rescinded, and that they be henceforth admissible conformably with the express declaration of right contained in the fourth section of the original Act of Parliament." This resolution was carried by twenty-four votes to eleven.*

The discussion which the above intricate question originated was carried on with much earnestness. A most full and masterly examination of the subject was made by the Rev. THOS. FALCONER, M.D., which received high legal commendation.

* The more this subject is examined, the more certain does it appear that the intention of the founders of the Hospital was to confine its benefits to " poor strangers."

Since this time the inhabitants of Bath have been admitted to the Hospital, though comparatively few avail themselves of the advantage, which indeed is not surprising when the facility for obtaining gratuitous baths afforded by the regulations established by the Corporation is taken into consideration.

On the 10th of May, 1832, a vacancy having occurred in the office of House Apothecary, Mr. HENRY JAMES PRINCE was elected to that situation. This occurrence only deserves notice from the fact that the gentleman then elected became well known from his connection with an establishment in Somersetshire called the "Agapemone."

In 1836, a legacy of £600 was left, duty free, to the Hospital by one who himself, as well as his father, had been always interested in the welfare of the charity—PRINCE HOARE.*

In 1840, a proposal was made to the Governors by FRANCIS H. FALKNER, Esq., one of the Vice-Presidents of the Hospital, to provide an exercising ground for the patients, by the purchase of the Bath Rectory House and premises, which it was understood was then for sale. The proposal was favourably received, and an offer made for the purchase of the Rectory House, which was declined. Out of this resolution, however, arose those beneficial alterations and additions to the Hospital which have recently been completed, greatly to the advantage of the patients and the better and more complete administration of the Charity, and of which a fuller account will be presently given.

---

* Prince Hoare was born in Bath, in 1755, and was educated as a sculptor, though better known as a dramatist.—Vide *Monkland's Supplement to " The Literature and Literati of Bath,"* pp. 51, 52.

Chapter II.

In 1842, the Hospital having been opened for a period of one hundred years, it was determined to issue a Centenary Circular setting forth the great advantages of this Institution. Fifteen hundred copies of this circular were distributed throughout the kingdom, several being sent "to every county in England and Wales, addressed to the Resident Ministers of the Parishes containing the largest population."

It was proposed at the same time to celebrate this period by making some addition to the accommodation for the patients, but no measures were taken in this direction.

At a General Court held on the 1st of May, 1843, amended By-laws were approved, and ordered to be submitted to the Lord Bishop of Bath and Wells, and the Justices of Assize for the county of Somerset, for their sanction, after which they were printed, together with an abstract of the Acts of Parliament relating to the Hospital.

In April, 1846, the Governors determined on publishing Annual Reports of the Institution. The only document which had up to this period been given annually to the public consisted of the names of the Officers and Governors of the Charity, together with an abstract of the Hospital accounts, the names of the Subscribers, and the laws by which the admission of patients were regulated. The first Annual Report was drawn up by the late W. SUTCLIFFE, Esq., and submitted to the President and Governors at their annual meeting in May of that year.

On the 1st of April, 1847, the attention of the Governors was a second time directed to the acquisition of the Rectory House and grounds, and a Sub-Committee was appointed to report on the expediency of their endeavouring to purchase this property. No report, however, was made; but the subject was fully considered in the annual report submitted to the Governors on the 1st of May. This report was received, and a motion made for the appointment of a Sub-Committee to ascertain the value of the property, and the adaptation of it to the purposes of the Hospital. This motion, however, was withdrawn, as the General Committee stated that it was not their intention to enter into any agreement for the purchase of the property without again bringing the subject before the General Court. Nothing more was done in the matter for more than two years, when in December, 1849, directions were given to renew the negociations for the purchase of the property. On the 20th of December, a letter was received from the solicitor of the Rector of Bath, in which a schedule of the property was given, and the purchase money definitely fixed at £3,700. On the receipt of this communication it was resolved, that "the purchase should be completed forthwith on the terms proposed." But on the 27th a second letter was received, "by which it appeared that a difficulty exists respecting the sale of the Rectory House, inasmuch as the Rector would be deprived of the income arising from the purchase money until it were re-invested in other property in the parish, for which he has at present no desire."

On the 4th of January, 1850, a General Court was

specially held to consider the proceedings which had taken place in reference to the purchase of the Rectory House, and also a letter from the solicitor for the estate, to the effect that arrangements might be made with the commissioners of "Queen Anne's Bounty," by which the alleged difficulty might be overcome, and suggesting an application to that body. This course was approved by a large majority. What took place between the above date and the 28th of November is not recorded, but on the last-named day directions were given for the payment of the costs of the proceedings for the purchase of the Rectory House and premises, and the Committee recorded their regret that the negociations for the acquisitions of the property had failed.

In 1851, in consequence of the Hospital accommodation being inadequate to meet the increased number of applications for admission, it was proposed that additional wards should be made on the western side of the Hospital, and estimates and plans were prepared. It was, however, very properly suggested that, as the outlay for this purpose would be large, it was desirable to relinquish the proposed plan, and endeavours made to obtain a site for the erection of a new Hospital. This view was adopted by a General Court of Governors on the 29th January, 1852, and on the 5th February, a site was submitted to them for consideration.

From this time until May 1st, 1854, the greatest activity prevailed in endeavouring to obtain an eligible locality for a new Hospital; the reports, letters, and negociations, were various and numerous, exhibiting an anxious desire to do whatever was in the power of the Governors to carry out their unanimous decision to remove the Institution to another situation. No less than six sites were brought under their consideration, namely, Sydney Gardens; a plot of ground near Manvers Street; land in St. James's Street, between Seymour Street and Norfolk Buildings; a portion of the Freemen's Estate, situated between the Victoria Park and Upper Bristol Road, below Marlborough Buildings; ground in the Villa Fields; and a site near the North Parade Bridge. The most desirable of the above sites, namely, the Sydney Hotel, could not be obtained by the Governors; the residents in the neighbourhood objected to the erection of a Hospital near them, and the owner of the property, Lord WILLIAM POWLETT,* yielded to their representations. In another instance the sum required was larger than the Governors considered themselves authorised to expend; in another, the difficulties in the transmission of the waters, and the distance from the spring, precluded its being selected.

One site seemed for some time likely to be determined on, namely, the portion above-mentioned of the Freemen's Estate; and considerable pains were taken to investigate the possibility of conveying the water with undiminished, or but slightly diminished temperature and unimpaired properties to that locality. On this subject a report was made by Professor MASKELYNE, of Oxford. But one important feature was omitted in the investigation, namely, whether at the proposed distance from the spring a sufficiency of water could be supplied for the Hospital Baths, without materially diminishing the quantity of water necessarily required for the King's Public Bath, and the adjoining private baths. Had this point been suggested for consideration, it would have been found at once fatal to

* Afterwards third Duke of Cleveland.

the removal of the Hospital to the Freemen's Estate.

At a General Court, held May 1st, 1854, the President and Committee reported to the Governors the reasons which induced them "to suspend all operations regarding the building of a new Hospital," which received the approval of the Court. The grounds on which this decision was founded were afterwards published in the form of a pamphlet, entitled, "A Brief Statement of the Reasons which induced the President and Governors of the Bath Mineral Water Hospital to decide upon retaining the Hospital on its present site, and upon purchasing the adjoining premises with a view to its enlargement."—May, 1858.

In 1855, on Thursday, the 15th of March, the following resolution was passed in consequence of an intimation that a large number of invalided and wounded soldiers returning from the Crimean war were about to pass through Bath, and which was highly creditable to the Hospital authorities, and is well worthy of being remembered :—" The Mayor of Bath (W. HUNT, Esq.) having undertaken to provide accommodation for one night (on Friday next), for one hundred and thirty of the sick and wounded soldiers from the Crimea on their way from Plymouth to Chatham ; it was resolved that the twenty beds in Queen's Ward be set apart for their use, and the men be supplied with a Dinner, Tea, Breakfast, and that every attention be paid to their comfort ; Major BAKER and Mr. MONKLAND undertaking to superintend the necessary arrangements."

A like praiseworthy arrangement was made by the authorities of the Bath United Hospital for the accommodation and entertainment of a second portion of the soldiers in that Institution, and a third portion was provided for at the Guildhall, the Banqueting Room in that building being converted for the time into a dormitory for the convenience of the soldiers.

In the early part of 1856, when it became known that the Hospital was about to be enlarged, an effort was made to incorporate Bellott's Hospital with the General Hospital; but some legal, as well as other obstacles, were raised, which prevented this desirable and beneficial arrangement from being carried into execution.

About the close of the same year, Government being desirous of trying the efficacy of the Mineral Waters in the treatment of several diseases to which soldiers are exposed during active service, application was made by the Director-General of the Medical Department of the Army for the admission of a limited number of soldiers. This was acceded to and several were admitted and occupied a ward in the Hospital for about a year. The result of this experiment, it is understood, was satisfactory; the number of soldiers who recovered and benefited by the use of the waters amounted to seventy-five per cent. of the number admitted.

In June of this year an opportunity presented itself of opening a fresh negociation with the late Rector, Bishop CARR, to purchase the Bath Rectory House and premises, was gladly embraced by the Governors, which eventually proved successful, though many difficulties presented themselves; in the same month a portion of the purchase money was paid, and the remainder in 1857, but it was not until May the 1st, 1857, that any decisive steps were taken to procure funds for the contemplated alterations and additions to the Hospital, on which day WILLIAM

LONG, Esq., commenced the subscription on his being elected President of the Charity; on which occasion, also, the late JAMES BRYMER, Esq., made a munificent donation, accompanied with a certain condition, which will be subsequently mentioned. From this time the Governors were occupied in considering different plans prepared by Messrs. MANNERS and GILL, and in making appeals to the whole country for funds to carry out the wishes of the Governors. Additional property in the neighbourhood was also bought, so as to give the fullest possible space for the contemplated arrangements.

After much deliberation by the Building Committee appointed to consider the subject, a plan was submitted to a General Court of Governors, on the 29th of December, 1858, by which it was proposed to erect a new and capacious building, connected with the present Hospital, to include two large Day-rooms (one for male and the other for female patients), a Chapel, Board-room, Rooms for the officers of the Establishment, etc., etc., with a convenient airing-ground for the patients. It was also proposed that when the building was completed, the old building should undergo rearrangement, the provisions for applying the Mineral Water should be improved, and the present board rooms and officers' rooms should be converted into wards. This plan, which was prepared by Messrs. MANNERS and GILL, received the unanimous approval of the Court, and was directed to be carried into execution. On the 14th of March, 1859, the work was commenced by pulling down the Rectory House. The removal of this and adjoining buildings, and the trenching ground for the foundation of the walls, occupied the time from March until the end of May when the work was sufficiently advanced to allow arrangements to be made for commencing the new building.

The 4th of June was fixed on for laying the foundation stone of the new edifice. Considerable interest was shown in this day's proceedings by the residents and visitors of Bath, and the citizens generally. The Mayor and Town Council, with the Members—W. TITE, Esq., and A. WAY, Esq.—and Magistrates for the city, assembled at the Townhall, where they were met by the President and Governors of the Hospital, the Lord-Lieutenant of the County, the Bishop of the Diocese and the Clergy, and also by a large number of influential gentlemen of the city and neighbourhood. A procession was formed, headed by the children of the Blue Coat Schools, which took the route of Cheap Street and Union Street to the Upper Borough Walls; at the junction of the last-named thoroughfares the road was spanned by an arch of evergreens bearing various inscriptions.

On arriving at the site of the intended building, which was enclosed and surrounded with galleries thronged with spectators, those forming the procession took up the places assigned to them; the Lord PORTMAN, the Bishop of Bath and Wells, the Mayor, the President, and the Governors, assembling near the foundation-stone. The proceedings commenced by the children of the Blue Coat Schools chanting the first and second verses of Psalm cxxvii., and the first, second, and third verses of Psalm xli., together with the *Gloria Patri*, at the conclusion of which the Bishop delivered the following prayer :—

"O God the Father, King of heaven and earth, by whom alone any work of charity can prosper, and who hast abundantly blessed the establishment of this Hospital for healing the sick and needy of our land, look favourably, we pray Thee, upon the undertaking we have this day commenced. Grant that this building, the foundation stone of which is now to be laid, may be for the further benefit of Thine afflicted poor. We know, O God, that no remedy can be effectual unless Thou blessest it. Bless, then, we pray Thee, the use of the waters of this city, and grant that they may be made powerful by Thee to restore health to the sick, as the pool of Bethesda was to give strength to the palsied. O Lord Jesu Christ, Son of the Father, who art the great Physician of souls, look favourably on the labours of those who shall be appointed to minister to the bodily cure of the inmates of this Hospital. Bless the means which they use to relieve the suffering, and strengthen the weak. May they look to Thee for guidance, acknowledging that to Thee belong the issues of life and death! O Holy Spirit, inspire and assist Thy servant, who is appointed to minister to the sick in holy things, and whom Thou hast appointed to watch for souls as one that must give account. Teach the afflicted to profit by his instruction, to do and to suffer Thy will, knowing that in Thy love Thou afflictest them. Make them to know that in whatsoever way they may be dealt with, Thy will is best for them, and may they cheerfully acquiesce in Thy dispensations! Incline the inhabitants of this city to be diligent in ministering to the necessities of those who may be sent here for the healing of the waters. Stir up those who are blessed with this world's goods to have pity on the sick and needy, and to give alms of their substance for the support and maintenance of this house of mercy for those who need the healing of these waters. Teach them to give bountifully, with cheerfulness and simplicity, as unto Thee, that they may, through Thy boundless mercy, be found amongst those to whom Thou wilt at last say, 'I was a Stranger, and ye took Me in; sick, and ye visited Me.' Grant these petitions, O Lord, for the glory of Thy Name, through Jesu Christ our Lord. Amen."

The Lord's Prayer was then said by the Bishop, and repeated by the assemblage.

The Right Honourable the Lord PORTMAN then proceeded to lay the foundation stone, first, however, placing two bottles into receptacles made for them in the nether stone; one of which contained seventeen coins of the present realm, including a five-sovereign piece, the gift of the late JAMES SNAITH BRYMER,

Esq.; the other the following statement engrossed on vellum :—

THE BATH GENERAL OR MINERAL-WATER HOSPITAL.

Incorporated by Act of Parliament, 1739.

The following statement comprises a brief account of the proceedings connected with the erection of the additional building to the Bath General or Mineral Water Hospital.

In the year 1840 it was thought to be desirable that an exercising ground should be provided for the patients of the Hospital, and for this purpose the Governors endeavoured to purchase the Rectory-house and premises of the parish of St. Peter and St. Paul, contiguous to the Hospital on its western side. The endeavour to purchase this property proved unsuccessful.

In 1847 negociations were renewed for the purchase of the Rectory, and continued until 1850, but were again fruitless.

In 1851 the accommodation for patients in the Hospital was found inadequate to meet the increasing number of applicants for admission, and suggestions were entertained for adding to the upper story of the Hospital, which were eventually relinquished.

In 1852 a proposal was considered to rebuild the Hospital on a new site; several localities were submitted for consideration both in this and the succeeding year, but various circumstances, and among them the impossibility of removing the Hospital to a distance from the Mineral Springs, prevented the adoption of any of them.

In 1855 the attempts to purchase the Rectory-house and premises above-mentioned were renewed, and this time with success, and in 1857 the purchase of this property was completed and various plans prepared and considered by the Governors.

In 1857, May 1st, a subscription for the erection of an additional building to the Hospital was commenced by WILLIAM LONG, Esquire, on his being elected President of the Charity.

In 1858, December 29th, at a General Court of the Governors, a plan on which it was proposed to erect the new building was adopted, which included day rooms, a chapel, a board room, and officers' apartments, etc.

In 1859, March 14th, the work was commenced by pulling down the Rectory-house.

On the 4th June, 1859, the first stone of the new building was laid by the Right Honourable the Lord PORTMAN, Lord-Lieutenant of the County, Custos Rotulorum, etc., etc.

The Lord Bishop of the Diocese, Lord AUCKLAND, assisted at the ceremony.

At this time WILLIAM LONG, Esquire, was President of the Hospital, and RANDLE WILBRAHAM FALCONER, Esquire, M.D., one of the Physicians of the Hospital, was Mayor of the City.

The Committee to whom the ordering and management of all matters relating to the new building and the alterations in the old one were delegated consisted of the following Governors :—The President for the time being; James S. Brymer, Esq.; David Johnston, Esq.; James Heywood Markland, Esq., D.C.L.; Jerom Murch, Esq.; George Monkland, Esq.; Randle Wilbraham Falconer, Esq., M.D.; and William Long, Esq. The Physicians and Surgeons of the Hospital were as follows :—*Physicians*—Thomas Sanden Watson, Esq., M.D.; Randle Wilbraham Falconer, Esq., M.D.; Charles Coates, Esq., M.D.; *Surgeons*—Richard Francis George, Esq.; George Leighton Wood, Esq.; John Stothert Bartrum, Esq. *Resident Apothecary*—Charles Terry. The Rev. W. A. Smith, M.A., Chaplain. Benjamin Starr was Registrar of the Hospital. Miss Charlotte E. Brooke, Matron. George Phillips Manners and John Elkington Gill were the Architects of the Building, and William Melluish, Clerk of the Works. God prosper the charitable undertaking.

These memorials were then covered by a brass plate bearing this inscription :—

"GOD PROSPER THE CHARITABLE UNDERTAKING."
The First Stone
of the
ADDITIONAL BUILDING
to the
BATH GENERAL or MINERAL WATER HOSPITAL,
Was laid on the 4th day of June, in the year of our Lord, 1859,
By the Right Honourable
THE LORD PORTMAN,
Lord-Lieutenant and Custos Rotulorum of the County of Somerset.
WILLIAM LONG, Esq., M.A., President.
BENJAMIN STARR, Registrar.
RANDLE WILBRAHAM FALCONER, M.D., Mayor.
GEORGE PHILLIPS MANNERS and
JOHN ELKINGTON GILL,
Architects.
WILLIAM MELLUISH, Clerk of the Works.

Chapter II.

Mortar having been spread, the foundation stone was slowly lowered to its appointed place, a band meanwhile playing the Hallelujah Chorus. This being done, the Lord PORTMAN went through the usual proceeding of trying the level, etc., of the stone, and finally striking it at each corner, saying as he did so, " I declare this stone to be duly laid in the NAME OF THE FATHER, OF THE SON, AND OF THE HOLY GHOST. AMEN." Then, turning to the audience, his Lordship spoke as follows :—

"I now certify to you here assembled that the foundation stone of what is intended to be an additional building to the Mineral Water Hospital is truly laid. I have had the honour of holding in my hand the trowel which was used more than a hundred years ago in laying the foundation stone of the other part of the building. May God bless the new building as it has pleased Him to bless the old one ! and may the bounty, the liberality, the good feeling, not only of the inhabitants of the county of Somerset, but of those of the adjoining counties, whose poor and afflicted are relieved by the waters of this city, contribute to complete this building in a way that is worthy the charitable feeling of this great nation. I am aware, as you all are doubtless aware, that a sufficient sum has already been contributed to justify the ceremony we are now going through ; but we all know that in the progress of works of this kind increased assistance is always wanted. I trust that that increased assistance will not fail to be rendered by those who live farther off from Bath than the inhabitants of the county of Somerset, and the county of Gloucester, and the county of Wiltshire, who send their patients here for the relief of the healing waters. I also trust that those who carry back to distant parts of England the recovered health and the benefits which the waters have afforded them, will induce, as they have induced, distant friends to assist in this great undertaking. It is one of the happiest things that can befall any one who holds her Majesty's commission, and who is the chief military officer of the county, to be called on to assist in inaugurating the new building. I am the more happy because I have associations with this great city of Bath. I have affections going back some generations. The fact that two relatives of mine were restored to health by the healing properties of your waters makes me particularly pleased to be called upon to officiate on this occasion. It has pleased God to bless this locality with healing waters, and it is the duty of man to make the best use of them, and to make them as beneficial to his fellow-creatures as he possibly can. I trust that what we have originated to-day will result in greatly increased benefit to those who suffer."

His Worship the MAYOR said:—"Mr. President, my Lords and gentlemen; as representing the municipal body and citizens of Bath, on this occasion, I trust that you will allow me to offer to you and the Governors of the Bath General Hospital, their and my own sincere and cordial congratulations on this auspicious commencement of a very charitable and valuable undertaking. I feel assured that the great body of the citizens of Bath are deeply interested in the welfare of an institution which ranks among the earliest established Hospitals of the kingdom—which is peculiar as respects the object which led to its foundation—and which admits within its portals, without distinction, the sick, and at the same time needy natives and residents of England, Scotland, Ireland, and the principality of Wales. Regarded in this last aspect, it is truly a national charity, and therefore it claims support from the whole of the United Kingdom. But though a national charity, it has its claims upon every citizen of Bath, inasmuch as it is the public and faithful exponent of the virtues and efficacy of those healing springs which it has pleased Providence graciously to place in this locality, and to which the origin, importance, and continued celebrity of this city are mainly attributable. As the custodians of the mineral springs, I hold it to be the paramount duty of every citizen to promote the means specially instituted for their employment, which duty cannot be more effectually fulfilled than by cherishing that Hospital which has been committed to their keeping by the piety of our forefathers. I cannot conclude without expressing my conviction of the obligations the citizens of Bath are under to the President of the Hospital. I know full well how anxiously, how zealously, how sincerely, he has endeavoured in every way to promote the prosperity of the Hospital, and especially the success of the present undertaking. But should the public be slow to recognize, as they too often are, such services, he has gained that which neither public approval nor public neglect can make or mar, the happy consciousness of having strenuously endeavoured to advance, for the sick poor of our common country, the welfare of an institution within whose walls his name will ever be kindly remembered by his associates, and can never be disconnected from the pleasing event of this grateful day."

The PRESIDENT, in addressing the meeting, said:—"My Lord Portman, my Lord Bishop, Mr. Mayor, ladies, and gentlemen,—One hundred and twenty-two years have passed away since the first stone of the adjoining building was laid by Mr. PULTENEY, afterwards Earl of Bath. Since the Hospital was opened for the reception of patients in

1742, 39,137 persons have been received within its walls, of whom 11,535 have been restored to their homes cured, and 19,293 relieved. With such abundant evidences of the wonderful virtues and efficacy of the Bath Waters in curing many diseases for which ordinary medical treatment might have been sought in vain, it was natural that the Governors should consider it their bounden duty to take advantage of the earliest opportunity that presented itself for enlarging and improving the Hospital. Through the kindness of Bishop CARR, the present Rector of Bath, the obstacles to the purchase of the piece of ground upon which we are assembled were overcome; the site was secured, and is now the property of the Governors of the Hospital. We have to-day commenced the great work of erecting the new building, and we look forward to its completion as a means of supplying the deficiencies of the present contracted building, and of providing accommodation for patients during the day-time (the want of which has long been felt), a chapel, board-room, and apartments, and new offices for the officials of the institution. I take this opportunity of stating that the present building will be converted into a dormitory for the inmates, and when re-arranged, not only will the comforts of the patients be increased, but we shall be able to provide twenty additional beds, which, if public liberality will enable us to fill them, will allow of nearly one hundred more patients being passed through the Hospital in the course of a year than can be done at present. Let us hope that the work which has this day been so auspiciously inaugurated by your Lordship, may be carried on to a prosperous conclusion. Let us hope that no *contretemps* may arise in the course of its progress, and that no accident may befall any one engaged in the erection of the building; but that in due time it may be satisfactorily completed and opened for the use and benefit of the patients. I am sure that, of all who are assembled upon the present occasion, none more cordially and heartily wish 'God speed' to our undertaking than your Lordship and the Lord Bishop of the Diocese, and in the name of the Governors of this Institution I beg to tender you our best thanks for attending here upon the present occasion, and for taking part in the ceremony of the day."

The singing of the Old Hundreth Psalm, and the pronouncing of the Benediction by the Bishop, brought these interesting proceedings to a close. As the numerous assembly dispersed, a collection was made for the Hospital Building Fund, which amounted to sixty pounds. In the afternoon, eighty gentlemen, consisting of members of the committee, governors of the hospital, and others who had joined in the proceedings of the day, were received by the President at a cold collation at the York House.

It should be mentioned that, on the morning of the day on which the foundation-stone was laid, a special meeting of the committee was held for the purpose of opening and deciding on the tenders for erecting the new building; and a contract was entered into with Mr. GEORGE C. MANN for the execution of the mason's, carpenter's and joiner's, plumber's, slater's and plasterer's, smith's, bell-hanger's, glazier's, painter's, paper-hanger's and gas-fitter's works, at the sum of £8,354. The warming and ventilation were entrusted to Messrs. HADEN AND SON, of Trowbridge.*

Having mentioned the names of those most prominent in advocating the interests, and contributing to the first establishment of the Hospital, it is only just to mention by name those who were among the principal contributors to the new building, namely :—H.R.H. the PRINCE OF WALES ; The Most Hon. the MARQUIS OF WESTMINSTER ; The Right Hon. the EARL MANVERS ; The Right Hon. the LORD PORTMAN ; JAMES S. BRYMER, Esq.;

---

* The names of those who were concerned in the erection of the new building are deserving of mention. J. Elkington Gill, Esq., architect. G. C. Mann was general contractor, and he executed the mason's work. His sub-contractors were:—Morgan and Lovell, carpenters; John Kerslake, plumber; Cook and Son, slaters and plasterers; G. R. Packer, glazier and painter; Haden and Son put up the warming apparatus; and H. Ezard, jun., executed the Carving in the pediment and in the chapel.

JOHN BRYMER, Esq.; JOHN BORTHWICK, Esq.; P. B. DUNCAN, Esq., LL.D.; T. H. KING, Esq.; WILLIAM LONG, Esq.; J. H. MARKLAND, Esq., D.C.L.; H. D. SKRINE, Esq.; W. TITE, Esq., M.P.; A. E. WAY, Esq., M.P.; Mrs. JOHN HILL; and Mrs. JAMES BRYMER.

The contributions, however, of JAMES SNAITH BRYMER, Esq., to the improvement of the Hospital, demands special notice. He gave One Thousand Pounds for a ward in memory of, and to be called "Archdeacon Brymer's Ward," after his late brother, the Venerable WILLIAM THOMAS PARR BRYMER, M.A., Archdeacon of Bath. In addition to the above, he gave £290 to the Building fund, and afterwards £500 for the special embellishment of the Chapel. These munificent gifts, as well as the interest which Mr. BRYMER manifested in the work, the completion of which he did not live to see—having died suddenly on the 1st of December, 1859—fully merited the following resolution, passed by the Committee shortly after his decease, namely:—
"*That the Committee, with deep sorrow, desire to record their sense of the great loss sustained by the sudden death of that munificent and much honoured member of their body*, JAMES SNAITH BRYMER, Esq.

"The earnestness with which he entered into every question affecting the welfare and prosperity of this Hospital; his constant and zealous attendance at the meetings of the Committee; the frank and cordial kindness of his manner; the especial interest he took in the erection of the new building; and the noble liberality by which he so materially promoted that undertaking, are fresh in the remembrance of every one.

"The providing a suitable place of Divine Worship was ever an object dear to his heart, and his gift of £500 will enable the Governors to meet his wishes by completing this in a manner befitting in all respects the House of God. This subject continually occupied his later thoughts, and as he had made provision for perpetuating the memory of his brother, the late Archdeacon of Bath, in connexion with one of the new Wards, so will the Chapel, which owes so much to his munificence, be ever associated with the memory of himself.

"It has pleased the Almighty Disposer of all things to call him home before he could see the termination of the work in which he was so deeply interested;" but in the words of the Annual Report (1859):—"So long as the new building shall endure, the lively interest which he ever took in its erection, and his large-hearted liberality, will not cease to be remembered in connexion with it."—*From the Annual Report for 1860.*

In consideration of these beneficent acts, and as an acknowledgment of personal regard and affection, the Governors, at their individual cost, have inserted into the southern wall of the ante-chapel, a window to the memory of Mr. BRYMER, which represents the incidents recorded in the parable of the Good Samaritan.

It will be remembered that on the 1st of May, 1857, WILLIAM LONG, Esq., commenced the subscription for the enlargement and improvement of the Hospital on being elected President of the Charity, which important office, by the unanimous choice of the Governors, he occupied for three years, during which time, the unwearied attention he devoted to the supervision of the progress of the new building, and the personal exertions he made to obtain funds for its successful completion, are deserving of great commendation, and fully justified the Quarterly Court of Governors, held on the 1st of May, 1860, when he retired from the office of president, in unanimously agreeing to the following resolution:—

"*At this meeting the Governors would express the deep sense which they entertain of the eminent services which have been rendered to this Hospital during the last three years, by their late President,* WILLIAM LONG, ESQ. *To his judicious and untiring labours are owing the wise arrangements by which a large amount of funds for the erection of the adjoining building has been obtained and the good progress which has been made in that fabric since the foundation-stone was laid. Their thanks must not be limited to one service, however important, as, during the lengthened period that* MR. LONG *has filled the President's chair, his faithful and punctual discharge of the several duties of his office, and his care and attention in promoting the best interests of the Hospital in* EVERY WAY *have been unremitting, and entitle him to the warmest thanks of his brother Governors, of the Subscribers, and the public.*"

In 1859, GEORGE KITSON, Esq., who had formerly held the office of Surgeon to the Hospital, died; and the following resolution, dated June 16th, of this year, deservedly commemorates his valuable services to the Hospital, and is worthy to be mentioned here:—

"*The Committee desire to record their sense of*

the loss they have sustained by the death of GEORGE KITSON, ESQ. He was elected a Governor in *1810*, and a Surgeon of the Institution, in *1817*. He held this later office, the duties of which he performed with zeal and close attention, for twenty-five years, during the greater part of which time he was associated with DR. BARLOW. After his resignation of this office, in *1842*, he continued, as governor, to take a lively interest in all that concerned the welfare of the Hospital, and his last public act in connection with it was to attend the ceremony of laying the first stone of the additional building on the 4th of June. The Committee gratefully recognise MR. KITSON'S long and valuable services in connection with this institution."

On the 1st November, 1860, a special meeting of the Committee was called by the President, " to consider the tenure of this Hospital under the Master and Co-Brethren and Sisters of St. John's Hospital, which would be materially affected by the scheme for the order and management of the charity after the decease of the present master, which it was understood would be submitted for approval to the Court of Chancery, by the Municipal Charity Trustees. It was stated that by this scheme no more renewals of lives would be permitted, but that the existing leases would be allowed to expire with the lives for which they are now held, depriving the Lessees of the right they were supposed to enjoy of perpetuating the holding, by renewing a life for a fine of one year's value,—a custom which had prevailed for a very long period, and on the faith in the continuation of which many improvements and bargains had been effected." As this proposal, if carried out, was considered as "liable to affect very injuriously the interests of the Hospital," a Sub-Committee was appointed "to consider and report to the General Committee, as to the steps it would be thought right to take." The Sub-Committee subsequently held a Conference with a deputation of the Municipal Charity Trustees, who, in consideration of the nature and importance of the Charity, consented to submit and recommend to the Charity Trustees the following proposal:—

"That a clause should be inserted in St. John's scheme to grant the fee of the site of the Mineral Water Hospital to the President and Governors, at a Ground Rent of Five Pounds, to be paid to S. John's for ever, and secured in the usual way, such ground rent to commence on the immediate surrender of the existing lease for three lives."

On the 29th of November, it was reported to the General Committee, "That the Bath Charity Trustees had, at their Meeting on the 20th inst., resolved to receive the report, and adopt the recommendation of their (the Hospital) Sub-Committee, with the addition 'that if the Hospital under any circumstances shall be removed from its present site, the site should revert to the Trustees of St. John's Hospital,' and that application should be made to the Charity Commissioners when they have power to do so."

On the 10th November of the same year, "*His Royal Highness the Prince of Wales was declared to have become a Governor of the Hospital, by virtue of a donation of One Hundred Pounds to the Building Fund, from the revenues of the Duchy of Cornwall.*"

On the 1st day of January, 1861, the following resolution was unanimously passed at a Quarterly

Court of the President and Governors of the Hospital, with reference to the decease of three Governors of the Hospital, two of whom, independent of their connection with the Charity, were well-known and esteemed by the citizens of Bath for many years:—

"*That this Meeting desire to record their deep regret at the loss of three of the Governors of the Hospital since the last Quarterly Court:—of* Mr. HALLIDAY, *whose useful services as a member of the Committee will long be thankfully remembered; of* Mr. NORMAN, *who filled the office of Governor for thirty-one years, and who in this, as in all other Institutions with which he was connected, displayed the kindness, the judgment, and ability to which his fellow-citizens have so abundantly testified at his funeral; and of* Mr. PHILIP GEORGE, *who for fifty years a Governor, during the greater part of that time legal adviser to the Hospital, and more recently a Vice-President, and who in all these relations,* BUT ESPECIALLY AS THE LEGAL ADVISER, *in which he evinced great judgment and liberality, obtained from his contemporaries, through various generations, their sincere respect, and will be deeply lamented with more than common sorrow, by all who are now attached to the Hospital.*"

Between this period and the assembling of the General Court on the 1st of May, nothing of more than ordinary interest occurred. By the report then presented, the Governors were informed that the architect stated that the whole of the new building would be ready for occupation about the beginning or middle of July, and the attention of the Court was directed to the arrangement which should be made for opening that building.

On the 27th of June, the BISHOP OF BATH AND WELLS and LORD PORTMAN, having intimated that it would be convenient to them to attend at Bath for the purpose of assisting at the opening of the new building, the 11th of July was fixed upon for the proposed ceremony. A programme of the proceedings was arranged, and Sub-Committees for carrying it out were appointed.

Chapter III.

On the 11th of July, 1861, a few days more than two years from laying the foundation-stone of the new building, it was opened for the reception of patients. In the morning of that day the President and Governors of the Hospital, with the Clergy of the City and neighbourhood, and several of their friends, met the Mayor and Town Council, and Magistrates, at the Guildhall, on leaving which, the following procession was formed:—

Hanoverian Band.
Blue Coat Schools.
Clergy.
Aldermen and Town Councillors.
Mayor's Officers.
Town Clerk.   The Mayor.   City Treasurer.
W. Tite, Esq., M.P.
Country Gentlemen and Visitors.
The Architects.
The Hospital Building Committee.
The Lord-Lieut.:   The President: The Lord Bishop:
Lord PORTMAN,   J. MURCH, Esq.,   Lord AUCKLAND,
The Rev. W. A. Smith & The Rev. J. C. Tasker.
The Governors of the Hospital.

The procession took the route of High Street, Cheap Street, Union Street, to the new building;

those officially connected with the Hospital, and their friends, proceeded to the Board Room, where were displayed numerous offerings for the Chapel, the Sacramental vessels given by Mrs. WILLIAM LONG; altar cloths and "fair linen," by Mrs. JAMES BRYMER; altar books by Mr. MACKARNESS; the Bible and Prayer Book for the Reading desk by Mr. MONKLAND; the altar chairs by Mrs. J. ELKINGTON GILL; seat and kneeling stools for the pulpit and reading desk by Mr. JOHN RAINEY; and an alms box by Mr. THOS. KNIGHT. The cushions at the altar and for the communicants were worked and presented by Mrs. J. BRYMER, Mrs. A. SMITH, Mrs. MARKLAND, the Misses PALMER, Miss MONKLAND, Miss CROSS, Miss BROWN, of Uley, and Mrs. and the Misses FALCONER.

The President, having taken the Chair, made a few preliminary remarks. The thanks of the Governors were then given to the donors of the offerings above enumerated, and the meeting proceeded to the Chapel. The prayers and lessons were read by the Hospital Chaplain, the Rev. W. A. SMITH, assisted by the Rev. J. C. TASKER; and the chanting was performed by a choir, directed by Mr. POND. The Sermon was preached by the LORD BISHOP OF BATH AND WELLS. At the termination of the service a collection was made for the Hospital Fund, which amounted to £129. After a brief interval, the public assembled in the men's day ward, known as Archdeacon Brymer's ward, when the President read an address, briefly recapitulating several of the more prominent facts in the history of the Hospital, setting forth its advantages, and indicating its possible effect on other localities where healing springs are found. After which the Mayor addressed the meeting in congratulatory terms upon the completion of the work, pointing out the usefulness of the institution, and enumerating the names of those who had aided in so commendable an undertaking, as the improvement and enlargement of so valuable a charity.

LORD PORTMAN then spoke at some length, referring first to the satisfaction he derived from assisting at the completion of a work, to the commencement of which he had contributed. He observed that he could have wished that he had on his right hand the Prince of Wales, " that he might have testified, as it was his wish to have done, his sincere desire to assist in the carrying out this great work of charity,—*the first great work of charity that His Royal Highness assisted from his own purse.*" He had every anxiety to come here, but the proposal was made to him at a time when it was impossible for him to set aside other engagements, which he had made for his summer occupation. His Lordship, in continuation, pointed out the benefits of the Hospital to the sick and suffering, and the claims which it has upon the whole community, and concluded by offering his congratulations on the successful efforts which had been made to erect the new building, and expressed a hope that future generations would do their utmost to preserve its efficiency and usefulness.

The LORD BISHOP of the Diocese availed himself of the occasion to address some well-timed and pertinent remarks to the patients and nurses of the Hospital, pointing out their individual and relative duties, and the true motives which should actuate the latter in their careful attendance on the sick.

The National Anthem was then sung, and a collection made for the Hospital Building Fund, from those who had not attended the service in the Chapel.

At the conclusion of these proceedings, a large number of the Governors and their friends were invited by the President to luncheon in the new Board Room, and brought the proceedings of the day to a close.

It is now necessary that the improvements added to the Hospital by the new building should be described.

The old and new Buildings are connected by a bridge-way on the first floor, supported by pillars, over Parsonage Lane, and below, by means of a tunnel under the same thoroughfare. A spacious hall and wide staircase occupy the centre of the ground floor. In the former is placed a bust of RALPH ALLEN, the gift to the Hospital of WARBURTON, having on a shield, attached to the pedestal, the following inscription :—

  RADULPHO ALLEN, O.V., AMICITIÆ GRATIA,
  H.M. PUB : POSUIT. GULS. WARBURTON.

On the right hand of the Hall is the Board-room, 32 feet long by 26 broad. This room contains numerous portraits of founders and benefactors to the charity, and some other paintings of interest connected with its object.* On the same floor is a waiting room,

---

 * The following is a list of the paintings, etc., which are placed in the Board-room of the Hospital :—
 Northern side.—Portrait of Dr. Frewin (Frewen ?) of Oxford, a benefactor, anno 1743.* Portraits of Mr. and Mrs. Roffey, benefactors

  * *See Notes and Queries*, 3rd Series, Part xxxii., p. 150.

rooms for the resident Medical Officer, the Registrar and Matron, Porter's Lodge, and the Dispensary.

On the left of the landing above, is the entrance

of £1000, anno 1770. Portrait of John Donne, Esq., a benefactor, 1750. Lithographic portrait of P. B. Duncan., Esq., President of the Hospital, 1849. Tablet recording Mrs. Wignall's legacy to the Hospital. A large painting by W. Hoare, Esq., Dr. Oliver and Mr. Peirce, physician and surgeon, examining patients afflicted with paralysis, rheumatism, and leprosy, anno 1742. Engraved portrait of Mr. Allen. Tablet commemorating the centenary of the Hospital. Illuminated copy of Latin verses, by the late Rev. F. Kilvert.

Western side.—A portrait of Ralph Allen, Esq., formerly in the gallery of Prior Park, presented to the Hospital by James S. Brymer, Esq., 1856. Plan of the Charmy-down estate, the property of the President and Governors of the Hospital, 1858. Portrait, by Mr. Gray, of Mr. W. B. Farnell, forty-four years apothecary to the Hospital, and a benefactor in 1829. List of Presidents of the Hospital.

Southern side.—Mrs. Morris, wife of the first apothecary to the Hospital, 1742. Mr. Morris, husband of the last named, anno 1742. Engraved portrait of Lieut.-Gen. Sir William Cockburn, Bart., N.S., formerly one of the vice-presidents of the Hospital. Engraved portrait of Caleb H. Parry, M.D., F.R.S., physician to the Hospital from 1800 to 1817. Engraved portrait of Edward Barlow, M.D., physician to the Hospital from 1819 to 1844.

Eastern side.—Portrait of Ralph Allen, bequeathed to the Hospital by the late Cap. Montagu Montagu, R.N. Portraits of Mr. and Mrs. Morris, father and mother of the first apothecary to the Hospital. Portrait, by Wm. Hoare, Esq., of Henry Wright, Esq., surgeon to the Hospital, 1742. Portrait of Richard Nash, M.C., 1742. Record of a bequest of £600, by Prince Hoare, Esq. Copy of Van Houe's map of Bath. Painting, by William Hoare, of Hygeia. Photographic portrait of Gen. Jervois, K.H., Colonel of the 76th foot, formerly Vice-President of the Hospital. Engraved portrait of Henry Harington, M.D. Photographic view of the laying of the foundation stone of the new building added to the Hospital. Portrait of W. Hoare, Esq., by himself, 1742. Portrait of Daniel Danvers, Esq., Treasurer of the Hospital 1760, by W. Hoare, Esq.

Bust of Ralph Allen in the entrance-hall. Busts of Mr. Peirce and Dr. R. W. Falconer on the first landing.

to the women's day room, which is 78 feet long, by 26 feet wide. On the opposite side of the landing, is the entrance to the men's day room, which is 70 feet long, by 43 feet wide. Both day rooms are 22 feet high; they are lighted by sun-lights in the evening, are warmed by fire-places and a warm air apparatus; and care has been taken to render the ventilation as complete as possible. They each have on the southern side, a balcony overlooking the exercise ground, which is laid out with gravel walks, and borders and shrubs. And, on its eastern side, an ample shed for the accommodation of the patients. In the men's day-room, which has been named ARCHDEACON BRYMER'S Ward, there is a plate attached to the northern wall, on which is engraved the following inscription :—

> ARCHDEACON BRYMER'S WARD.
> THE LATE JAMES SNAITH BRYMER, ESQ., GAVE
> ONE THOUSAND POUNDS
> TOWARDS THE ERECTION OF THIS BUILDING, ON CONDITION THAT
> A WARD SHOULD BE NAMED IN MEMORY OF HIS BROTHER,
> THE VENERABLE THOMAS PARR BRYMER,
> LATE ARCHDEACON OF BATH, CANON OF WELLS,
> AND FORMERLY PRESIDENT OF THIS HOSPITAL.
> OPENED JULY XI. MDCCCLXI.

The chapel, which owes so much of its beauty to the late JAMES BRYMER, ESQ., is highly creditable to the architect, the late J. ELKINGTON GILL, ESQ., and to MR. H. EZARD, JUN., the carver, working under the architect's direction. On the left hand of the entrance to the Chapel, a circular brazen plate is inserted into the wall, bearing the following inscription :—

†

THE LATE
JAMES S. BRYMER, ESQ.,
PRESENTED FIVE HUNDRED POUNDS
TO BE SPECIALLY APPLIED
TO THE HOLY ADORNMENT OF THIS CHAPEL,
FOR THE PROMOTION OF
THE REVERENT WORSHIP OF
ALMIGHTY GOD,
1859.

On the opposite side is a stained-glass window, representing a tree, with a label bearing the following texts :—

"*I was glad when they said unto me, Let us go into the house of the Lord.*"

"*Create in me a clean heart, O God, and renew a right spirit within me. Purify me with hyssop, and I shall be clean: wash me and I shall be whiter than snow.*"

On the right hand side of the ante-chapel is the memorial window, erected by the President and Governors of the Hospital, to the memory of the late J. S. BRYMER, Esq., in which are represented the incidents described in the parable of the good Samaritan. In the lower compartment, the good Samaritan is pouring wine and oil into the wounds of the traveller. In the middle he has placed the wounded man on his own beast; and in the upper, he is providing the host, with the sum for the support of the sufferer, who is reclining on a bed. Above the upper department is the text, "*Whatsoever more thou spendest, I will repay thee.*" And below the lower compartment, the following inscription:—

TO THE GLORY OF GOD,
AND
IN MEMORY OF JAMES S. BRYMER.

The whole is encompassed by a vine bearing grapes, beyond which is an ornamental bordure.

Opposite to this window is an organ made by Sweetland, of Bath, which was purchased by subscription, and erected in the chapel, by permission of the President and Governors of the Hospital, on the opening of which, on the 3rd of December, 1862, three special services were held, and collections made, which amounted to £53 3s. 10d.

The ante-chapel is divided from the Chapel by three arches. The caps of the pilasters are finely carved, each representing a different subject—the water buttercup, the wild poppy, three fish, the fig-tree, two birds drinking from a cup, the pomegranate, the phœnix and the pelican, being here used for decorations.

The five two-light windows in the southern wall are also of stained glass. In the tracery at the top of each, a coat of arms is inserted, viz., the arms of the Brymer family, the Bath arms, the Royal arms, the Prince of Wales's arms, and the arms of the See of Bath and Wells. The caps of the centre shafts and of the Devonshire marble columns on the sides of these windows, are carved with the serpent and the apple; thorns and thistles; the vine and lily; the passion flower; palm and crown; the pomegranate and trefoil.

The apsis is lighted by seven circular-headed windows, the subjects in these all refer to Scriptural incidents connected with water, viz.: the baptism of Jesus by St. John Baptist; Christ at the pool of Siloam, healing the sick; Christ washing the feet of His disciples; the baptism of the Eunuch by St. Philip; Christ and the woman of Samaria at the well; Naaman the Syrian in the waters of the Jordan; and Moses striking the rock.

The caps of the marble columns of these windows exhibit carved emblems of the Passion—the chalice, the crown of thorns, the cross with the passion flower, wheat and grapes, the spear, hyssop, and scourge, the hammer and pincers, and the nails. The crown of apsis is coloured blue and spangled with stars, with rays of glory, the rays being carved in stone. The arch itself is supported by four columns of marble, on the caps of which are carved symbols of the Four Evangelists. The soffit of the arches is enriched with panels, and the arch in front has the passion flower, finely sculptured in bold relief.

The pulpit is of white lias from Clandown. The corbel supporting the pulpit is formed of two storks elegantly sculptured, surrounded by bulrushes. The three panels forming the body of the pulpit have the monogram I.H.S., a Maltese cross, and an emblem of the Trinity carved on them. The caps of the columns are carved representations of the rose and lily, the delicate and excellent workmanship of which are deserving of special attention. The reading desk is an eagle, carved in oak.

The panelled ceiling is enriched with boldly rendered mouldings of the white lily, and the four transverse beams are adorned with olive branches.

Around the walls of the chapel, immediately underneath the cornice, there are selections from the *Te Deum* in red letters on the stone :—

"*We praise Thee, O God: we acknowledge Thee to be the Lord.*

"*All the Earth doth worship Thee: the Father everlasting.*

"*To Thee all Angels cry aloud.*

"*To Thee Cherubin and Seraphin: continually do cry,*

"*Holy, Holy, Holy: Lord God of Sabaoth.*

"*Heaven and Earth are full of the Majesty: of Thy Glory.*

"*The Holy Church throughout all the World: doth acknowledge Thee.*"

The corbels which support the four beams of the ceiling, consist of figures of sacred characters :— St. Peter, with an extract from the *Te Deum*, painted on the ribbon in red letters, "THE APOSTLES PRAISE THEE;" St. John the Baptist, with "THE PROPHETS PRAISE THEE"; St. Stephen, with "THE MARTYRS PRAISE THEE;" David with his Harp, with "PRAISE THE LORD UPON THE HARP;" Moses the High Priest, with "OH YE PRIESTS, BLESS THE LORD;" and Three Archangels, with "OH, YE ANGELS, BLESS YE THE LORD;" "PEACE ON EARTH," and "GLORY TO GOD IN THE HIGHEST."

The floor of the ante-chapel and other parts of the chapel are paved with red and black encaustic tiles. The chapel is twenty-five feet by fifty-five feet; will accommodate 150 worshippers; and is furnished with substantial open benches made of oak.

During the excavations for laying the foundation of the new Building many Roman remains were discovered, comprising large portions of a tesselated pavement of plain pattern, much earthenware, and coins of the Lower Empire, together with a fragment of an inscription on a marble slab, which possesses considerable interest. An account of the latter, with a list of the coins, earthenware, and bronze and bone implements found in the locality indicated, are given by the Rev. Prebendary SCARTH, in vol. XI. of "The Proceedings of the Somersetshire Archæological and Natural History Society." These remains were, on the 12th June, 1862, directed to "be handed over to the Corporation of the City, to be kept with other Roman Antiquities in the Literary and Scientific Institution, with the understanding that a separate case be provided for them, and a catalogue made to identify the locality in which they were found." *

On the 25th of July, the first General Court of Governors was held in the new Board-room, on which occasion the Court, in consideration of the efficiency, long services, and probable increase in the duties of the Registar, Mr. B. STARR, augmented his salary from £105 to £125 a-year; and, in consideration of the special services rendered by him in relation to the new Building, presented him with a gratuity of Twenty Pounds.

* Among these remains is a fragment of an inscription on a *marble slab*, which is deserving attention on account of its rarity in this country. A tesselated pavement, which was discovered about the same time, has been retained *in situ*, in the basement of the Hospital, so as to admit of being easily examined. The work, entitled "Aquæ Solis," by by the Rev. Prebendary Scarth, contains a full account of the remains of Roman Temples, Villas, Altars, Coins, &c., discovered in Bath and its neighbourhood, to which reference may be made for a description of the remains disclosed when excavating for the foundations of the Hospital.

Chapter III.

On the 12th of December, the Rev. W. A. SMITH resigned the office of Chaplain of the Hospital, after having discharged its duties for four years "*with*"—as expressed in the resolution passed on his retirement—"*the greatest credit to himself, satisfaction to the Committee, and benefit to the patients.*" The Rev. J. C. TASKER was elected to the office of Chaplain thus vacated, on the 27th of the same month. On the same day it was unanimously decided that an address of condolence should be prepared, and forwarded, by the President, through the proper authorities, to H.R.H. THE PRINCE OF WALES, on the decease of H.R.H. THE PRINCE CONSORT. The reception of this address was duly acknowledged by Major-General R. BRUCE, Private Secretary to H.R.H. the Prince of Wales, on the 4th of February, 1862.

On the 30th of January, 1862, the last portion of a considerable legacy left by Mrs. WIGNALL became the property of the Hospital, the history of which is briefly recorded as follows, in a tablet hung in the Board-room :—" This tablet is placed here by the desire of the Executrix of the late Mrs. Ann Wignall, of this city, for the purpose of recording a legacy bequeathed to this Hospital by that lady, of thirteen thousand three hundred and thirty-three pounds six shillings and eight pence, consolidated three per cent. annuities, contingent on the death of Susannah Tubb, Edith Lyne, Harriet Bennett, and Charlotte Burgess ; one fourth of the above sum being directed by her will, to be transferred on the death of each of the above parties.

" N.B.—£3000 consolidated 3 per cents. were transferred the 6th of December, 1830, to the President and Governors of this Hospital, by Mrs. Elizabeth Mackey, the Executrix, on the death of Charlotte Burgess above named, £333 6s. 8d. stock having been sold to pay the legacy duty thereon. A second £3000, in March 1850, on the decease of Harriett Bennett. A third £3000, in February, 1854, on the decease of Susannah Tubb. The fourth £3000, in May, 1862, on the decease of Edith Lyne."

In July, 1845, Mr. WILLIAM SLACK died, and by his will, proved on the 6th August, 1847, he left a sum of £50, to be annually paid to the Hospital; this sum has been so paid up to the end of the year 1861, but in 1862, it appeared that though it had been regularly paid by his representatives, the source from which it was derived was unequal to the continuance of the payment, and some legal difficulties arose which necessitated an application to the Court of Chancery, the decision of which has not yet been delivered.*

In July, the contemplated alterations and improvements in the old Building were commenced. In August, the number, of patients were diminished, in order to facilitate the progress of the alterations, which were completed in November, and the usual number of patients was again admitted.

The alterations here alluded to consisted in the conversion of the old Board-room and officers' rooms into dormitories, the enlargement of one ward, and the admission of a greater amount of light into all the dormitories, by splaying the windows, and substituting plate glass for the ordinary glass; the

* Has been decided, as may be seen in chapter IV.

construction of lavatories, reclining baths, vapour baths, etc. By these and other means, the defects of the old building have been removed and space gained for additional beds. As by the alteration of the old building, there was a new ward made, it was determined that it should be called "PERRY'S WARD," to commemorate Dr. WILLIAM PERRY'S munificent bequest to the Hospital, to which allusion has been already made.

During this year, the decease of GENERAL JERVOIS, an old Governor of the Hospital, is thus noticed in the proceedings of the Committee:—"The Committee, in recording the death of GENERAL JERVOIS, K.G., a Vice-President, and one of the oldest members of their body, desire at the same time to place on record their deep sense of the loss the Bath General Hospital has sustained in the death of a Governor, held in such deserved respect and esteem. Connected with the Hospital for a period of twenty-five years, GENERAL JERVOIS ever took a strong interest in all that concerned its welfare; and the remembrance of his warmth of heart, and of his unwearied kindness and courtesy, will ever be cherished here as elsewhere, by those who enjoyed the privilege of his friendship." At a later period a very admirable photographic portrait of GENERAL JERVOIS was presented to the Hospital, by his nephew, T. F. W. WALKER, ESQ., a Governor of the Hospital, and was placed in the Board-room.

On the 12th of February, it was resolved to solicit H.R.H. the PRINCE OF WALES to be nominated President of the Hospital. The application was made in due form, but was unsuccessful, upon which the Bishop of the Diocese, LORD AUCKLAND, was elected President for the year, on May 1st, 1863.

On March the 10th, being the wedding day of H.R.H. the PRINCE OF WALES, with H.R.H. PRINCESS ALEXANDRA OF DENMARK, the Hospital, in common with other public buildings of the city, was illuminated.

On the election of the Bishop of the Diocese to the office of President, on the 1st of May, 1863, the services of the retiring President, who had held that office for three successive years, during which time the new Building had been finished, and opened for the reception of patients, and the alterations and improvement in the old Building brought to a successful completion, were thus acknowledged by the unanimous approval of the Court:—"That the best thanks of the Governors be presented to JEROM MURCH, ESQ., for the courtesy and constant attention which he has devoted to the wants and necessities of the Institution, during the important period of its history, in which he has held the office of President."

Chapter IV.

ANNUAL MEETING,
May 1st, 1864.
J. Murch, Esq., President, in the chair.

The Committee reported that the increased accommodation provided by the enlargement and alteration of the Building, had enabled the Governors to admit a greater number of patients than had ever before passed into the Hospital in one year. The statistical tables show that 35 per cent. of these have been perfectly cured and upwards of 30 per cent. much relieved, which bears a very fair comparison with the returns of previous years, while the average stay of the patients in the Hospital has been shortened, thus realising the hopes entertained of the beneficial results arising from the introduction of day rooms and exercising ground, by means of which a more perfect ventilation of the sleeping wards during the day had been obtained, and thereby justifying the very large expenditure which has been incurred in the late improvements. The accommodation provided is for 85 males and 57 females.

The expenditure which has been incurred in the erection of the new buildings has obliged the Governors to draw rather largely on their capital, thus causing to some extent a diminution of their permanent income. The Committee have therefore directed their attention to the probable necessity of seeking some more profitable mode of investment for the funded property of the Hospital, and a special meeting was convened on the 3rd March, for the purpose of taking this important subject into consideration; at the meeting it was deemed advisable to take the opinion of counsel as to the power of the Governors to change the mode of investment; and they instructed Messrs. FALKNER, solicitors to the Hospital, to prepare a case to be laid before the Attorney-General, from whose opinion it appears that the Governors have the power of varying the investment in any manner they may deem advisable; it will therefore rest with the General Court to decide what mode or modes of investment will best combine increased profit with safety.

The income of the past year amounted to £4,031 3s. 8d.; the expenditure to £4,086 6s. 11d., showing an excess of expenditure of £55 3s. 3d., but this includes a sum of £133 19s. 8d. paid from the capital to the Building Fund. £343 14s. 8d. have been received from Donations and £45 by a Legacy from the late Sir CLAUDE WADE.

The house at the end of Old Bond Street has at last been removed, admitting a considerable amount of light and air to the old part of the Hospital, to the great benefit and comfort of the patients. The Committee have to lament the deaths of several of the oldest Governors of the Hospital—PHILIP BURY DUNCAN, Esq., and Lord MIDLETON, both of whom had been many years on the Committee and had both served the office of President; of Dr. JOHN FORD DAVIS, who was formerly a Vice-President and had been a Governor since 1809, and who had also been Physician to the Hospital for 17 years; and the Rev. F. KILVERT, who had been a Governor for nearly 40 years; also G. F. Bush, Esq., and the Hon. P. S. Pierrepont.

The Report of the Committee with the Financial Statement for the year was read and approved.

The following resolution was then passed:—" That the Committee be authorised with the sanction of of a general Court previously obtained, to vary the Investments from time to time as they may deem advisable, in accordance with the opinion of Counsel, but subject to certain restrictions recommended by the Committee."

The thanks of the Governors were voted to the Physicians and Surgeons for their valuable services during the year, and to the Rev. J. C. W. Tasker for the zealous and satisfactory discharge of the duties of his sacred office of Chaplain.

J. H. Markland, Esq., proposed and G. Monkland, Esq., seconded the nomination of Major Baker as President for the ensuing year. Carried unanimously.—J. Murch, Esq., proposed that the best thanks of the Governors be given to the Lord Bishop of the Diocese for acting as President during the past year. Mr. Markland seconded the resolution, which was carried unanimously. Major Baker returned thanks for the honour conferred upon him in electing him President for the ensuing year.

ANNUAL MEETING,
May 1st, 1865.

Major Baker, President, in the chair.

The Committee reported that many advantages had

arisen from the enlargement of the Building, and the construction of an exercise ground, as shown by the increased number of Patients that have derived benefit from the Hospital. In 1858, previous to the alteration, the number discharged were 512, whereas in 1865 the numbers were 632, a strong proof that increased space and means of obtaining air and exercise, had tended greatly to a more speedy cure of the Patients. The income of the past year did not cover the expenditure. The President had sent appeals to 14 parishes and unions in London and its vicinity, selecting those that had been in the habit of sending the largest number of Patients, and setting forth the very strong claim which the Hospital had on them for support, but the Committee regret that only 3 unions have recognized those claims. The income of last year amounted to £4,047 14s. 3d. and the expenditure £4,124 14s. 11d. Of the income £345 16s. was derived from private subscriptions; £504 7s. from parochial unions; £193 1s. 3d. from collections in churches in Bath; £422 15s. 4d. from donations; and £90 from legacies.

The Committee have to lament the loss of some very valuable friends of this Institution, viz. :— JAMES HEYWOOD MARKLAND, Esq., who had been 22 years a Governor, 12 years one of the Treasurers, and had filled the office of President during three successive years; THOMAS HARPER KING, Esq., who had been twice elected President, and had been for many years an active member of the Committee; Sir JOHN FRASER, a Governor of four years' standing, and a constant attendant at the Meetings of the Committee; Dr. EDWARD HODGES, formerly a

Physician to the Hospital, and the Rev. E. W. GRINFIELD, all elected Governors; also JOHN FRANKHAM, Esq., ROBERT NORRIS, Esq., and ROBERT HITCHENS, Esq., Governors by donation.

The Committee have also to regret the loss of MALMOTH WALTERS, Esq., who has resigned the office of Governor on account of ill-health.

The Report of the Committee, with the Annual Insurance Statement, was read and adopted. The best thanks of the Governors were voted to the Physicians and Surgeons, for their valuable services during the year, and to the Rev. J. C. W. TASKER, for the jealous discharge of his duties as Chaplain. The Governors also expressed their approbation of the way in which the several officers of the establishment had discharged their respective duties. On the motion of Col. BLATHWAYTE, seconded by the Mayor of BATH, DAVID JOHNSTONE, ESQ., was unanimously elected President for the ensuing year. A vote of thanks by acclamation was given to the retiring President, MAJOR BAKER, for his great courtesy and attention to the interests of the Hospital during the past year.

ANNUAL MEETING,
May 1st, 1866.

David Johnstone, Esq., President, in the chair.

The Committee reported that there was a diminution in the number of Patients admitted during the past year, which was accounted for by the alterations, at present in progress, necessitating the temporary closing of some of the wards, and also by the prevalence of small pox, requiring the appropriation of two wards to a possible emergency which the new sick wards will entirely obviate for the future.

At the period when the new Building was in course of erection, the intention of the Committee had been to erect sick wards ; the great expense which would be incurred and the proposed erection implying the removal of the roof of the old Building caused this project to be deferred. The want of sick wards, however, was so much felt that the Committee decided on carrying out their original intention, having however obtained the sanction of the Governors at a special Court. They gave necessary instructions, and the improvements were carried out under contracts amounting to somewhat more than £1000.

Donations amounting to £286 14s. 6d. had been received during the year. The Committee also reported that they had directed their particular attention to their position in conection with St. John's Hospital, consequent on a decision of the Lords Justices, that the Attorney-General was at present engaged in preparing a scheme for the future management of that Charity, and the Committee have reason to believe that the claims of the Hospital would be attended to.

During the year the following Governors were removed by death :—REV. JAS. PHILLOTT, REV. G. A. BAKER, REV. HARVEY MARRIOTT, and MISS ABRAHAM.

ANNUAL MEETING,

May 1st, 1867.

David Johnston, Esq., President, in the chair.

The number of patients admitted during the past year was considerably below the average number, the causes of this diminution having been entirely exceptional. On the recommendation of the Medical Staff, the admission of patients last summer was suspended until such time as the epidemic of small pox should have disappeared. Also during the whole summer and greater part of the autumn several of the wards were of necessity closed, on account of the alterations which were being carried out in the old house.

The whole cost of the new roofing, the new sick wards, and other improvements, has been £1,164. The Men's Bath, from which there had been a considerable leakage, was completely renovated: the lining of slate removed and replaced with lead, like the Women's Bath, which had been in use 20 years without requiring repairs. The Committee were glad to state that these great extra expenses have been nearly covered by a legacy of £1,068, left to the Hospital by the late Captain MONTAGU MONTAGU, R.N. The income of the last year amounted to £5,236 18s. 7d., the expenditure to £5,113 10s. 11d. The donations amounted to £470 4s. 4d., and legacies were left to the Hospital to the amount of £1,168 17s. The Committee have to lament the death, during the past year, of F. H. FALKNER, Esq., one of their Vice-Presidents and a Governor for 42 years, the Marquis CAMDEN, K.G., and the Rev. Dr. STAMER. The following Governors, by donation, have also died: Col. THORNTON, G. P. MANNERS, Esq., W. C. TOWERS, Esq. Dr. BURNE, having resigned, has ceased to be a Governor. Moved by Sir THOMAS PRATT, seconded by Mr. MONKLAND, and carried by acclamation, that the Governors, in accepting the resignations of THOMAS SANDON WATSON, M.D., senior physician, and GEORGE LEIGHTON WOOD, Esq., senior surgeon, desire to place upon record their grateful sense of the services rendered by those gentlemen to the Hospital, the former for the space of 33, the latter of 31 years. In parting with them in their professional capacity, the Governors rejoice that they shall still continue to have their counsel and advice in all matters that affect the interests of an institution, to the high character of which they have so largely contributed. With every wish for their happiness and welfare, the Governors accept their resignation, and now place this minute on record as an evidence of their esteem.

The vacancy on the Medical Staff, caused by the resignation of Dr. WATSON, was filled up by the election of Dr. JAMES TUNSTALL, and that in the Surgical Staff by the election of Mr. J. K. SPENDER. On the motion of Col. BLATHWAYT, seconded by Capt. BRETON, R.N., the Right Hon. the Earl of CORK was unanimously elected President for the ensuing year. The Mayor having taken the chair, Col. BLATHWAYT moved a vote of thanks to the late President, DAVID JOHNSTON, Esq., and also begged leave to give way as senior Vice-President, and recommended the newly-elected President to place Mr. JOHNSTON at the head of the list, so that the Institution might have the benefit of his services as Chairman in the absence of the President. Carried by acclamation.

ANNUAL MEETING,
May 1st, 1868.
David Johnston, Esq., Vice-President, in the chair.

The Committee reported that the expenditure had somewhat exceeded the income for the past year. The Committee acknowledged gratefully the following donations:—Marquis of WESTMINSTER, £100; C. H. WALKER HENEAGE, Esq., £10; Mrs. E. W. BROWN, £10. The following legacy was received: £99 19s. There was no diminution in subscriptions; these for the first time exceeded £900. The Committee regretfully reported the death of three elected Governors—Major PICKWICK, H. SNOWDEN, Esq., G. C. TUGWELL Esq.; by resignation, H. WALTERS, Esq. The Resident Medical Officer, Mr. J. COOKE, having resigned, Mr. H. CLOTHIER was elected to fill that important office.

The Rev. J. C. W. TASKER having resigned the Chaplaincy, the Rev. E. LANE was elected in his stead; and on the motion of Major BAKER, seconded by Dr. JAMES WATSON, the Rev. Prebendary SCARTH was unanimously elected President for the ensuing year.

WILLIAM LONG, Esq., proposed a vote of thanks to DAVID JOHNSTON, Esq., for the able, courteous, and efficient manner in which he had performed the duties of senior Vice-President, in the unavoidable absence of the Noble President, the Earl of CORK, which was carried unanimously.

ANNUAL MEETING.
May 1st, 1869.
Rev. Prebendary Scarth, President, in the chair.

The Committee reported that a larger number of patients had passed into the house than in any previous year since the house had been opened. Donations amounting to £240 10s., including £200 from the Marquis of WESTMINSTER, were gratefully acknowledged. Several reversionary legacies had been received, as well as bequests, also the sum of £438 from the Economic Life Assurance Society, payable on decease of the late THOMAS FALKNER, Esq. These extraordinary receipts not only covered the deficiencies of several years, but enabled the Treasurers to add £1,400 stock to the invested capital, besides leaving a larger balance in hand than at the commencement of the year. The Charmy Down Estate, held by Mr. G. MATTHEWS, as yearly tenant for 24 years, had been let to his son at an advanced rent of £36. The rent in future to be £450.

In October the Governors were sorry to receive the resignation of Dr. TUNSTALL, one of the Physicians to the Hospital, in consequence of failing health. Dr. HENSLEY was elected to fill the vacancy. During the year death had removed from the list of Governors Admiral WALCOT, M.P., and FRANCIS FALKNER, Esq., the able and much respected Solicitor to the Hospital, also THOMAS HARVEY, Esq. At this meeting Mr. JOHN FALKNER was appointed Solicitor to the Hospital, in the room of his late brother, MR. FRANCIS FALKNER. On the motion of Col. BLATHWAYT, seconded by the Rev. J. F. MOOR, HENRY DUNCAN SKRINE, Esq., was unanimously elected President for the ensuing year. A vote of thanks, moved by JEROM MURCH, Esq., and seconded by W. C. KEATING, Esq., to the late President, was carried by acclamation.

ANNUAL MEETING,
May 2nd, 1870.
H. D. Skrine, Esq., President, in the chair.

The Committee reported that the amount of subscriptions, which 20 years ago averaged £540, had now reached £920 per annum.

Donations altogether amounted to £315 19s. 6d. Legacies (free of duty) had been received as follows: Executors of the late Mr. JOHN VAUGHAN, Raby Villa, £100; Miss MARY HULBERT, Queen Square, £50; and Mrs. FRANCES DOWN, £100. The Committee regretted that by the decision of the Court of Chancery, this, as well as many other Charitable Institutions in the city, would no longer derive benefit from the will of the late Mr. WILLIAM SLACK. The personal property, which the court decided was alone liable, amounted only to about £7,000, and was nearly exhausted by payments made to annuitants for 15 years; the Hospital is now only entitled to one-eighth of the remainder, or £99 9s. 1d. The income of the year exceeded the expenditure by upwards of £100, notwithstanding an extraordinary expenditure of about £170 on the Charmy Down

Estate. Intermixed with the Charmy Down Estate are 32 acres of land belonging to the adjoining Hartley Estate, which the Governors had, at different times, sought to purchase. At present there appeared to be an opportunity of purchasing, and the Committee reported that they had entered into negotiation about it. The Committee reminded the Governors that in 1865, when the Corporation of Bath endeavoured to obtain an Act for the better supply of water to the city, which Act would enable them to take surplus water from certain springs, and some small quantity of land for the construction of reservoirs on the Charmy Down Estate, the Governors did not oppose the measure, taking care to protect and provide for the interests of the Hospital. That bill was not passed, but another was now before Parliament to which the Governors gave their assent under the same conditions. The subject of tenure of the old Hospital had also occupied the attention of the Committee. Being held on lease under St. John's Hospital for two lives, it was thought highly desirable, considering its proximity to the source of the Mineral Waters, that the Institution should have a more certain and independent foundation. Various attempts had been made with the view of obtaining from the Court of Chancery a conveyance of the fee-simple from St. John's Hospital, but hitherto without effect, and a Sub-committee had been appointed to consider whether a further offer should not be made and to what amount.

The Committee have to regret the loss of W. M. PINDER, Esq., JOHN MACKARNESS, Esq. and the Rev. FOUNTAIN ELWIN, causing three vacancies in the list of Governors. The Hospital had also sustained a great loss in the death of the late Marquis of WESTMINSTER, who had for many years aided the Hospital by liberal and frequent donations; also more recently in the death of Lord AUCKLAND, late Bishop of Bath and Wells, who had always taken a kindly interest in the Hospital and its affairs. The Governors, at their last Quarterly Court, had, by a resolution entered on the Minutes, expressed then their sense of his kind and valuable services and their sympathy with his Lordship and his family under the afflicting circumstances of his ill-health and sufferings, which had compelled him to resign his see. This resolution had been communicated to his Lordship by the President, and warmly and gratefully acknowledged by his daughter. JOHN STONE, Esq., and EDWIN SKEATE, Esq., have become Governors by donation. The Committee wished to express their grateful acknowledgement to Mr. JOHN RAINEY for his continued liberality in providing a choir for the Sunday musical services in the chapel, and also for his having generously contributed to the relief and amusement of the patients, by providing several evening entertainments for them during the past winter.

The report having been read, it was moved by the MAYOR of BATH, seconded by Rev. J. WOOD, that it be accepted, printed, and circulated; that copies be sent to every Governor and Subscriber, and to the officiating clergy in Bath. Moved by Major BAKER, seconded by G. BURNINGHAM, Esq., "That this Court entirely concurs with the Committee in their expression of sorrow for the loss of those Governors whom death has removed during the past year, particularly of the late Lord

AUCKLAND, whose warm and personal exertions in the welfare of this Institution are fresh in the memory of all." On the motion of D. JOHNSTON, Esq., seconded by J. MURCH, Esq., the Lord Bishop of Bath and Wells, LORD ARTHUR HERVEY, was unanimously elected President for the ensuing year. A vote of thanks to H. D. SKRINE, Esq., for his efficient discharge of the duties of President during the past year was carried by acclamation.

ANNUAL MEETING,
May 1st, 1871.
Col. Blathwayt in the chair.

The Committee had to report a falling off in Subscriptions, as also in Collections in Churches and Chapels. This diminution might be attributed to the pressure on behalf of newer Institutions and also to the generous aid afforded to the sick and wounded during the late disastrous war.

The Committee had to thankfully acknowledge donations amounting to £962 10s. 6d., including 12 Foreign Bonds from an anonymous donor, estimated at the price of the day at £687, also legacies amounting to £125. The Committee had received as the result of the Chancery suit in "*re* Slack's annuity," £99 9s. 1d. as the share due to the Hospital, and £66 16s. 3d. returned legacy duty.

The Committee had availed themselves of an opportunity of improving the Charmy Down Estate, by the addition of some land greatly needed for the purposes of the farm. On this object was expended altogether £1,700. The annual rent of the estate at this time was about £500.

Six elected Governors have died during the year :—John Brymer, Esq., W. C. Keating, Esq., Rev. Prebendary Crawley, John Soden, Esq., Col. J. W. Watson, and Rev. Sydney Widdrington. The following Governors by donation have also died :— G. Monkland, Esq., T. Brassey, Esq., Rev. W. Anderson Smith, and Arthur Edwin Way, Esq. This obituary list contains names long known and highly esteemed. Moved by J. Murch, Esq., seconded by D. Johnston, Esq., that the Committee be authorized to renew the negotiations for the purchase of the fee-simple of the old building, and if they deem it advisable, they be empowered to make an advance on the price already offered and refused as insufficient. This resolution was carried.

In regard to future Election of Governors it was ordered " That in the notices of the Quarterly Court, to be holden in January, it be stated how many vacancies have occurred in the list of Elected Governors, and that a book be kept for the entry of names of Governors proposed to fill such vacancies."

On the motion of the Rev. C. R Davy, seconded by General Hall, His Grace the Duke of Beaufort was unanimously elected President for the ensuing year.

ANNUAL MEETING,
May 1st, 1872.
J. Murch, Esq., Vice-President, in the chair.

The Committee reported that owing to some falling off in casual benefactions, expenditure had exceeded income by £314. The Committee also reported that with respect to the important point mentioned in former reports, of obtaining the freehold of that part of the Building held on lease under St. John's Hospital for two lives, it was arranged that two of the Governors, Mr. MURCH and Mr. STONE, should proceed to London for the purpose of obtaining an interview with the Attorney-General, and explaining the exceptional nature of the case. Their interview with Sir ROBERT COLLIER was most satisfactory. He soon after gave orders that the application should be granted on the payment of £1,200, being £300 within the sum allowed by the General Court at their last Annual Meeting. The transaction would be concluded in a few days, and the Committee congratulated the friends of this great National Charity on the circumstances that this whole range of Buildings will then be entirely free.

On the motion of Mr. Burningham, seconded by Mr. Skrine, Rev. Chas. Kemble was unanimously elected President for the ensuing year.

ANNUAL MEETING.
May 1st, 1873.
Rev. Preb. Kemble, M.A., President, in the chair.

The Committee of Governors, in their report to the General Court, announced with great satisfaction, the completion of the negotiations, which had been carried on for several years, for the fee-simple of the old Building of the Hospital, previously held on lives under St. John's Hospital.

For this purchase and attendant expenses £1,312 8s. 10d. was realized by the sale of Stock, and the Governors will in future have the satisfaction and gratification of feeling that they now occupy their own freehold.

The Chaplain, Dr. Lane, resigned in August, 1872, and the Rev. Thos. Tyers was elected in his room. On October 31st some difficulty having arisen as to the distribution of the Offertory Alms collected in the Hospital, the following arrangement has been made by the Chaplain with the approval of the Bishop:—
"That the offertory and alms collected at the Chapel be applied, at the discretion of the Chaplain, to the relief of poor patients on leaving the Hospital, and that there be placed before the Governors at the Quarterly Meetings, an account of sums received and cases relieved." There was also an account opened at the Savings Bank under the designation of the "Samaritan Fund," the purpose of which was nowhere defined. In order to prevent doubt as to the proper application of the Fund, a Resolution had been adopted, almost identical with that relating to the offertory and alms, excepting that the Chaplain should place his statement of application of these funds before the Governors once a year instead of quarterly.

The Committee reported with great regret the death of Sir Wm. Tite, through which this Hospital, as well as many other Philanthropic Institutions, have suffered a sad loss. Sir Wm. Tite became a Governor by donation in 1858. For 15 years his unvarying courtesy and liberality deservedly won the respect of all members of the board.

Two vacancies had occurred on the Board, by the deaths of Robert Aylwyn, Esq., and Lieut.-General Hale. A legacy of £500 has been left to the General Hospital by the late Miss Waldron, of Trowbridge, a name by which this Institution is generally known. The Committee and Trustees, however, of the Royal United Hospital have made a claim to the legacy, on the ground that the title given in the will was a clerical error. Under these circumstances the executors have decided to pay the legacy into the County Court, for a resolution of the doubt thus raised.

Resolved, that in order to prevent litigation in the matter of Miss Waldron's legacy, the following gentlemen be requested to place themselves in communication with the Trustees and Committee of the Royal United Hospital, in order if possible to attain that object:—Mr. Skrine, Mr. J. Johnston, and Mr. James Rainey. On the motion of Mr. Skrine, seconded by Major Baker, Major Ralph Shuttleworth Allen was unanimously elected President for the ensuing year. A vote of thanks was moved to the Rev. Prebendary Kemble, for his valuable services during the past year, and carried by acclamation.

ANNUAL MEETING,
May 1st, 1874.

Major Allen, M.P., President, in the chair.

The Committee reported that the income of the Hospital had been again inadequate to meet the increased expenditure caused by the higher price of provisions and other circumstances, and at the last Annual Meeting it was referred to the Committee to consider the desirableness of altering the investments, so as to obtain a larger amount of interest thereon. In June it was considered necessary to sell out £700 to meet current expenses, and since then the Committee, with the sanction of the General Court, have sold the whole of the remaining £40,400 Consols, and re-invested proceeds in the most approved Indian and English Railways, and Russian and Dutch Bonds, thereby increasing the income to £463, which it was hoped would prevent a further diminution of Capital. The Committee reported with regret that the settlement of the rival claims of the two Hospitals, to the legacy of the late Miss Waldron, could not be settled without litigation. This Hospital has been so long known as the General Hospital, and has received and continues to receive so many legacies and contributions under that designation, that the Governors could not forgoe their claim to this bequest, but under the circumstances would be willing to divide it. A legal decision, however, was found to be unavoidable, and after a careful hearing the Judge of the Bath County Court pronounced in favour of this Hospital, the cost of both parties to be paid out of the legacy, at the suggestion on behalf of the Governors.

As suggested at the last Annual Meeting, during the visits of the Royal Horticultural Society and the Church Congress, circulars were largely distributed with the view of making the Hospital and its objects more widely known, and to add to its funds. The Committee believe that the former object has probably been attained, but that very little has been added to the finances. During the past year vacancies occurred in the list of elected Governors, by the lamented decease of Wm. Carey Hope, Esq., W. H. P. Gore-Langton, Esq., M.P., and Rev. R. M. Boultbee, all of whom were liberal subscribers. The Committee have also to deplore the loss of Thomas A. Poynder, Esq., and W. M. Canning, Esq., both generous benefactors, and of John Elkington Gill, Esq., the esteemed Architect under whose plans and superintendence the new building was erected.

The Marquis of Bath was unanimously elected President for the ensuing year. On the motion of the Marquis of Bath, a vote of thanks was passed by acclamation to the President for his valuable services during the past year.

ANNUAL MEETING,
May 1st, 1875.
Jerom Murch, Esq., in the chair.

The Committee reported that they were thankful to be able to report various favourable circumstances during the past year. The income of the year, in consequence of the large amount of legacies, exceeded the expenditure by £606; on the other hand, the larger number of patients admitted, the high price of fuel and provisions, and some unavoidable repairs, made the expenditure £213 more than that of last year. The Committee received the following legacies:—Miss Waldron, deducting expenses of litigation, £344 12s. 8d.; Mr. Walter Tucker, £450; Sir W. Holburn, Bart., £100; The Marchioness of Thomond, £100; W. Stuckey, Esq., £19 19s. 0d.; Mrs. Henney, £5. The favourable state of the income is also due to the re-investment, as noticed in former reports, and sanctioned by General Courts, of the property of the Hospital formerly invested in Consols. From time to time the securities now held are looked into by the Treasurers, who now report that they are satisfactory. The Committee regretted the very great diminution in the amounts, once so large, raised by collections in the different Churches and Chapels in Bath. In common with all the charities of Bath, this Hospital has met with a great bereavement since the last Annual Report, by the death of the Rev. Prebendary Kemble, Rector of Bath, who filled the office of President not long since, and whose valuable services, as Vice-President, will long be remembered by those who acted with him. Great also was the loss of Col. W. Baker, who lately took an active part as Treasurer. The Committee also regretted the death of the following Governors :—Admiral Gawen Roberts Gawen ; Rev. H. Calverley ; Chas. Hoare, Esq. ; Mrs. E. W. Browne; and Mrs. Jones Bateman. Mr. Kemble was an *ex-officio* Governor, and would be succeeded by the Rector of Bath. The following have become Governors by donation :—G. D. Wingfield Digby, Esq., of Sherborne Castle, who has kindly consented to fill the office of President for the ensuing year ; Andrew Durham, Esq., and Mrs. James S. Brymer. The Committee could not conclude without expressing their sincere regret at the resignation of Dr. Coates and Mr. J. S. Bartrum, who have rendered most efficient services through many years, and whose places the Governors would now have to fill.

" Resolved, that this Court, being the first which has been held since the death of Col. Wyndham Baker, desires to record its sense of the loss sustained by the Hospital through his death, and during recent financial arrangements his assistance is especially to be remembered ; and that this resolution be sent to Mrs. Wyndham Baker, with an assurance of the sincere sympathy of the Governors in her bereavement." Dr. A. Beaufort Brabazon was duly elected Physician, in the room of Dr. Coates, resigned; Dr. Richard Carter was duly elected Surgeon in the room of John S. Bartrum, resigned; G. D. Wingfield Digby, Esq., was unanimously elected President for the ensuing year. A vote of thanks to the retiring President was carried by acclamation.

ANNUAL MEETING,
May 1st, 1876.
Jerom Murch, Esq., in the chair.

The Committee reported that the number of patients admitted during the past year was 776, somewhat less than that for the previous two years, but considerably larger than in former years. The income had been insufficient to meet the expenses by £158 10s. 2d., although £462 17s. 5d. had been received in legacies. It should be mentioned that the expenditure exceeded that of last year by £195 8s. 0d., chiefly in consequence of two cottages having been built on the Charmy Down Estate at a cost of £150. The legacies were:—from Mrs. F. Heywood, £200; Miss Eleanor P. Garrett, £50; Rev. Wm. Wills, £50; Mr. George Cottle, one-fourth of the residue of his estate, £162 17s. 5d. From the last legacy the Hospital would not derive full benefit. It was represented that on Mr. Cottle's death-bed, he had expressed his desire that his widow should receive a larger annuity than that provided by his will, which would have absorbed the whole of the residue. The Committee therefore resolved that £5 per annum should be granted to her out of the interest of the share falling to the Hospital. As stated in last year's report, the Church and Chapel collections in Bath had so fallen off, that it was resolved not to pray for their continuance where there was a reluctance to grant them. It was, however, gratifying to find, that some clergymen considered that so valuable a charity should not be altogether deprived of an important and much needed source of income, and kindly pleaded its cause as heretofore. The amount collected was, in the City Churches £94 8s. 3d., collections made in the Country Churches amounted to £47 6s. 10d.

During the past year the Institution had been deprived by death of the following elected Governors, whose places would have to be filled at the General Court :—S. Snead Brown, Esq. ; R. Perfect, Esq. ; Geo. Vivian, Esq. ; Admiral Dickson ; and H. W. Rideout, Esq. ; also of G. H. W. Heneage, Esq., and the Rev. H. E. Howse, who became Governors by donation. The latter was the oldest Governor on the list, having filled the office 56 years. It was to be earnestly hoped that the loss of such men, both to the finances and management of the Hospital, would be made up from time to time by the accession of new friends. James Watson, Esq., M.D., was unanimously elected President for the ensuing year.

ANNUAL MEETING,
May 1st, 1877.

Dr. James Watson, President, in the chair.

The Committee, in making their usual Annual Report, had the satisfaction of stating that, during the past year, the Hospital had continued to carry out the benevolent intention of its founders and supporters. The Financial statement was not unsatisfactory, although the receipts from ordinary sources had not been sufficient to meet the expenditure by £146 3s. 10d. This was to be attributed chiefly to heavy bills for necessary internal and external painting, to the last portion of the expense of building cottages on the Charmy Down Estate, and to an abatement of £25 made to the tenant of the farm on his rent. As, however, £150 of the Patients' Caution Money has been placed in the hands of the Treasurers in trust, the balance at the Bankers is £3 6s. 2d. more than at the commencement of the year.

The amount of annual subscriptions exceeded that of any former year, being £1,001 4s. 0d. The Church collections realised only £100 16s. 11d. The collections at 28 Country Churches amounted to £65 5s. 9d. Among the donations received were the following :—Miss Hicks and Miss Frances Hicks, in memory of their mother, Mrs. Anne Theresa Hicks, £100 ; The Earl of Jersey, £50 ; Honourable Julia Dutton, £40. These benefactions being severally to the amount of, or exceeding £40, the donors became Governors of the Hospital.

On the motion of Colonel Cockell, seconded by Major Baker, a vote of thanks was unanimously passed to the President, Dr. James Watson, for his kind and valuable services in the past year, and he was then re-elected President for the ensuing year.

Assent was given to a suggestion of Mr. Rainey, to allow the Committee of the Fine Arts Exhibition to have the loan of any of the Pictures belonging to the Hospital they may desire, at the coming Agricultural Meeting.

ANNUAL MEETING,
May 1st, 1878.
Dr. James Watson, President, in the chair.

The Committee again reported that the Institution continued steadily to perform its useful work and extend its benefits to distant parts of the kingdom. The Annual Subscriptions had been £978 8s., less than last year by £22 16s. The casual benefactions had also decreased, having only amounted to £129 2s. 4d. The collections at Bath Churches amounted to £104 12s. 4d., and at ten Country Churches to £27 3s. 6d. Fortunately, no extraordinary expenditure had been incurred during the year. The following legacies had been received: Mrs. Hinton, £1,000 (less duty); Mrs. Landon, £200; Mr. Henry Knight, £25; Miss Jackson, £25. The Committee pointed out that, without these legacies, expenditure would have exceeded receipts by £800, showing how much this noble institution depends on that very uncertain source of income. Donations amounted to £128. Death had during the year removed from the lists of Governors Chas J. Vigne, Esq., and T. F. W. Walker, Esq., both of whom had long been active and useful members of the Committee, and also Charles T. Maud, Esq. The Committee had to deplore also the death of Mrs. Hinton, who had long been a subscriber. She became a Governor by virtue of her frequent donations, and by her will bequeathed the munificent legacy already mentioned.

Also of the late Marquis of Ailesbury, who had been a subscriber since 1858, and who had lately become a Governor by donation. On the motion of Major Baker, seconded by General Eden, a vote of thanks was unanimously passed to the President, Dr. James Watson, for his kind and valuable services during the past year, and he was then re-elected President for the ensuing year.

ANNUAL MEETING,
May 1st, 1879.
Major Baker, Vice-President, in the chair.

The Committee reported that the number of patients admitted had been 783, 20 less than last year. Daily average in the house had been 126, and their stay 59 days. The cost of each occupied bed, £40 11s. 7d. During the summer of the past year, Bath was visited by the British Medical Association. The Committee were desirous that the Members should judge for themselves, so far as the Hospital would enable them to do so, of the nature and effects of the far-famed Springs. A considerable number of gentlemen availed themselves of the invitation, and were very much interested.

The Annual Subscriptions amounted to £1,058 17s. 0d., but the legacies and collections in Churches and Chapels at Bath have been considerably less. The legacies have been left by Mrs. Maxwell Hinds, £200; T. F. W. Walker, Esq., £100; Mrs. Clarke, £5. The Committee regard with great concern the inadequacy of the regular sources of income to meet the demands on the Hospital, and are doing all in their power, by appeals, both to individuals and Boards of

Guardians, to obtain increased Annual Subscriptions, and to prevent the necessity of the sale of Government Stock to meet deficiencies. It should also be known that the income of the Hospital had been reduced by an unavoidable reduction in the rent of the Charmy Down Estate. Foremost among the losses by death had been that of the venerable President, Dr. James Watson, in the third year of his Presidency and 86th year of his age. How efficiently he performed the duties of his office until within a few weeks of his death, will long be remembered by those who had the pleasure of being associated with him in the work which he loved. At the first General Court after his death, the Governors elected Mr. Murch, the senior Vice-President, to fill the vacancy for the remainder of the year. The other Governors by election who have died during the year were :—F. Falkner, Esq.; Colonel Inigo Jones; Captain H. A. Kennedy; Sir W. Miles, Bart.; and General Sir T. S. Pratt, K.C.B., who was also a Vice-President. Mrs. Duncan, a Governor by donation, also died. Dr. Spender resigned his appointment as Surgeon to the Hospital; his valuable services during 12 years have been thankfully acknowledged by the Committee.

Moved by Mr. D. Johnstone, seconded by Mr. F. B. Gill, that the Treasurers be instructed to sell out the following securities held by the Hospital :—The Russian Stock, the Indian Railway Stock, and the Dutch Government Bonds, and invest the proceeds in the best English Home Securities.

Moved as an amendment by Mr. J. Stone, seconded by Major Allen, that it is not expedient to sell the securities recently purchased except the Russian securities, and as regards them it be left to the Committee to do so at such time as they may think desirable. The amendment on being put to the vote was lost, 14 for and 24 against. The original motion was then carried, 19 for and 16 against. On the motion of Admiral Conolly, seconded by Captain Breton, R.N., Major Allen was unanimously elected President for the ensuing year. A vote of thanks was passed to the late acting President, Alderman Murch.

ANNUAL MEETING,
May 1st, 1880.

Major Allen, President, in the chair.

The Committee congratulated the Governors, that notwithstanding the general depression which had existed during the year, this Institution had maintained its reputation for usefulness and had received its usual support. The number of patients had been 854, or 71 more than the previous year. Daily average in Hospital, 124; the cost of each occupied bed, £40 0s. 7d., including all the expenses of the Hospital; Annual Subscriptions amounted to £1,061 7s. 7d.; Donations amounted to £276 7s. 7d., including the Right Honourable Stephen Cave, M.P., £50; Henry Chas. Stone, Esq., £40. The legacies, besides the long-pending reversionary bequest of the late Mr. Thomas Blann of £7,933 19s. 1d. Consols, which has been paid through the Court of Chancery, were :—Miss Mary Jeans, £200; Miss Ann Bolt, £90; Sir Thos. Chas. Style, Bart., £24 8s.; Miss Mary Cross Close, £15; General Hind, £50. The resolution of the Governors, at the last Annual Court, to dispose of the whole of the Foreign and Indian

Railway Stock, and to re-invest that part of the capital in *Home* Securities, had been carried into effect. The amount thus realised was £16,597 8s. 1d., of which £16,500 was re-invested in the purchase of Debenture and Preferential Stock of British Railways. In consequence of the occurrence of a case of small-pox, it was considered necessary to close the largest ward for five weeks. This one case was removed to the Statutory Hospital, and no other case occurred. In consequence of extensive alterations at the King's Bath, which interfered with the supply of the mineral waters for bathing patients in the Hospital, the Committee had been obliged to make an arrangement which may continue for some time for sending them to the public baths. Applications for the office of Registrar, vacant by the resignation of Mr. Benjamin Starr, were received, and on a ballot being taken, Mr. Frederick W. Dingle was duly elected. The following letter from Mr. Starr to the President was read, and ordered to be entered on the minutes :—

" Bath Mineral Water Hospital ;
April 30th, 1880.

SIR,—

In relinquishing the office of Registrar, it is a pleasing duty to present, through you, my most sincere and respectful thanks for the uniform kindness I have experienced from the Governors of the Hospital,—a kindness which has rendered the performance of the duties a pleasure ; and it is most gratifying to me, in this my eightieth year, to reflect that I have spent so long a portion of a long life in the service of so excellent a Charity.

I trust it will not be considered inopportune if I briefly allude to the progress the Institution has made during the time I have held office, by comparing the year 1840 with the present year.

In 1840 the number of patients which passed through the Hospital was 524. It is now 854. The amount of annual subscriptions was then £526. This year it was £1,061. The total income in 1840 was £3,871. Now it is nearly £5,000. Upwards of £20,000 have also been invested in the site and erection of the new building, and in the purchase of the fee simple of the old building and its improvement.

With an ardent desire that the Institution may still advance in prosperity and usefulness, and continue to be the best advertisement of the efficacy of the Bath Mineral Waters, and thus promote the interest of my native City,

I beg to remain, with great respect, Sir,
And many thanks for your courtesy,
Your very obedient Servant,
BENJ. STARR.

Major Allen, President."

The usual routine business having been disposed of, on the motion of Major Baker, Major Allen was unanimously re-elected President for the ensuing year, with the best thanks of the Governors for his past services.

ANNUAL MEETING,
May 1st, 1881.
Major Allen, President, in the chair.

The Committee reported that full evidence was afforded that the Hospital continued steadily to fulfil the benevolent desires of its founders. Last year it was reported that, owing to alterations at the King's Bath, patients would be unable to bathe in the Hospital, and that arrangements were made for their bathing in the Public Baths, for many reasons, and from the fact that it was found that the patients did not derive the benefit which they would have derived, had they bathed in the Hospital, and considering also the expense of conveying the patients to and from the Hospital, it was deemed a good opportunity to have the inside of the Hospital thoroughly painted, which had not been done for many years, and it was therefore decided (July 15th) not to admit any more patients, but gradually discharge those in the house. Five weeks afterwards (Aug. 23) the buildings were given into the contractors' hands, and in six weeks the work was completed and the Hospital re-opened Oct. 2nd. As a matter of course, the number of patients admitted has been less than last year, being 765. The Annual Subscriptions amounted to £1,070 9s. 6d. The Donations have been £215 2s. 4d., including that of Lady Victoria Howard, £40, and Wm. Stone, Esq., £40. During the past year one legacy of £2,000 has been received from the executors of Miss Mary Wasey, though, from the language of the will, it was at one time a question whether the claim of the Hospital might not have to be asserted by appealing to a Court of Law. The generosity of Messrs. Cotterell Brothers, of Bridge Street, in decorating the ceiling of the Entrance Hall of the Hospital, should also be mentioned. During the year the following Governors have been removed by death: Edwin T. Caulfeild, Esq., Right Hon. Stephen Cave, M.P., R. T. Combe, Esq., and F. L. Popham, Esq., all liberal contributors to the funds of the Hospital, and Governors by virtue of their benefactions; also of Rev. Preb. Pearson, for many years a Subscriber, and Governor by election.

On the motion of Mr. Burningham, Major Allen was again re-elected President for the ensuing year, and the best thanks of the Governors presented to him for his past services. The following notice was appended to the Annual Report:—

"Whilst this Report was being prepared for the press, the Hospital has had the misfortune of losing its Senior Physician, Dr. Randle Wilbraham Falconer, and at a meeting of the Committee it was unanimously resolved:—'That the President be requested to convey to Mrs. Falconer the deep sympathy of the Committee in the great bereavement she has sustained.' For 25 years Dr. Falconer has assisted in the management of this Institution, and for the whole of that period he has given his talent and energies ungrudgingly and without stint. As one of the Honorary Physicians, the kind and sympathetic feeling which he showed for the poor and suffering must, it is felt, meet with its due reward, and the tribute from the Female Patients in sending a wreath to be placed on the coffin bears testimony in a gratifying and consoling manner of their estimate of his tender care for them."

ANNUAL MEETING,
May 1st, 1882.
Major Allen, President, in the chair.

The Committee reported that the applications for admission had been above the annual average, the largest number of patients on record having been received into the Hospital, viz., 879. Donations, with smaller sums, amounting to £102 17s. 2d., including £40 from John F. M. H. Stone, Esq., and £40 from E. S. Fletcher, Esq., were thankfully acknowledged. Five legacies had been received, amounting to £274 12s. 4d. This was the smallest amount received in legacies for the past nine years. This year the expenditure had exceeded the income by £237 18s. 5d. A portrait of the late James

Snaith Brymer, Esq., a Governor and liberal contributor to the funds of the Hospital, had also been bequeathed by Mr. John Rainey. It has been found desirable to increase the temperature of the Hospital, and the Committee, in consequence, had erected a hot-water apparatus, which has greatly contributed to the comfort of the patients. The Committee have to thank Dr. Brabazon, the Avon Rowing Club, and the Bloomfield Cricket Club, for kindly giving Musical Entertainments to the patients.

The thanks of the Governors are also due to Mr. James Tuck Rainey, for the handsome altar rails erected in the Hospital Chapel, in memory of his brother, the late Mr. John Rainey, who, until his health failed, took so warm an interest in the welfare of the institution. At a General Court, held on May 30th last, Dr. J. K. Spender was elected Physician in the room of the late Dr. Randle Wilbraham Falconer, and Mr. Alexander Busby to the post of Resident Medical Officer.

Mr. Jerom Murch having taken the chair, it was proposed by Mr. Burningham and seconded by Mr. John Johnston, and unanimously resolved, that the best thanks of the Governors be awarded to Major Allen for his past valuable services, as President of the Hospital, and that he be requested to assume that office for the ensuing year.

ANNUAL MEETING,
May 1st, 1883.
Major Allen, President, in the chair.
The Committee, in presenting their report, have

much pleasure in stating that, during the past year, more patients had been admitted than in any previous year. The great increase in the number of applicants shows that the Hospital, and the efficacy of the Bath Mineral Waters, are more known and more widely appreciated than formerly. The number of applicants for admission had increased from 961 during the year ending May, 1881, to 1,280 in the past year. The grand total admitted within the walls of the Hospital since its opening in 1742 has been 56,131.

"The daily average in the Hospital has been 130, and the average duration of residence a little less than that of previous years, being $48\frac{3}{4}$ days. Many of the cases always have required, and always will require, considerable time, but it is interesting to observe that (as was anticipated when contemplating the erection of the new building) a larger number of patients pass through the Hospital annually since the time they have been enabled to remove into fresh, airy, and cheerful day rooms, and at night return into well-ventilated bedrooms; and, as the applications for admission greatly exceed the accommodation, it is now thought that if a room for recreation is added to the Hospital and the patients not allowed out of the precincts during their stay, thus obviating the temptation to visit public-houses (and thereby retarding their recovery), a still larger number will be benefited.

"The Committee have therefore made an offer to purchase of the Trustees of St. John's Hospital the premises known as 'The Sedan Chair Inn,' immediately abutting upon the Exercising Ground, and the contract is now in the hands of the Charity Commissioners for their approval."

The income arising from vested capital, and from

the uncertain sources of subscriptions and benefactions, amounted to £4,625 19s. 4d., insufficient to cover the year's expenses by £407 9s. 8d., increased as they have been by the high price of provisions and the large number of patients treated in Hospital. The Committee had therefore been reluctantly obliged to sell out stock to meet the deficiency. The annual subscriptions from private persons amounted to £428 19s., and from Union and parishes £726 16s. Donations amounted to £304 19s. 4d., including the following:—Rev. J. Buttanshaw, £25; Earl of Jersey, £10; Mrs. C. A. T. Luttrell, £50. The collections at churches and chapels in Bath again decreased this year, producing £68 13s. 3d. The clergy in the country parishes responded to an appeal made to them, and collected £92 15s. 5d. Under the head of legacies only £9 has been received. Owing to the large number of fires which have occurred in various parts of England, the Committee have purchased additional hose and appliances to insure the greater safety of the patients in case of need.

The Committee at this anniversary have to record with deepest sorrow the losses which this charity has sustained during the past year by the deaths of several Governors, but principally by the decease of General W. Eden and John Johnston, Esq., the former a Vice-President and for upwards of 18 years a member of the Committee, and the latter also a Vice-President, Treasurer, and for nearly eighteen years a member of the Committee.

Three other vacancies in the list of elected Governors are caused by the deaths of the Hon. Howe Browne, R. Hudleston, Esq., and by the resignation of Colonel T. A. Rawlins.

The Committee have also to deplore the loss by

death of Mrs. Browne and R. W. Carpenter, Esq., both liberal contributors, and who became Governors by virtue of their benefactions.

The following gentlemen were elected Governors of the Hospital:—W. E. Brymer, Esq., General Gordon Jervois, Col. Reginald Quinten Mainwaring, E. J. Morres, Esq., and the Rev. E. T. Stubbs. The General Committee, Sub-Committees, and Treasurers, were appointed for the ensuing year.

Major Allen returned thanks for the assistance he had received during his presidency from the Governors and Officers of the Hospital. The chair was then taken by Major Baker, Vice-President. It was moved by Mr. Burningham, seconded by Mr. Duckworth,— That the warmest thanks of the Governors be tendered to Major Allen for his constant attention to, and the constant interest he has taken in this National Charity; also for the able manner in which he has performed the duties of President during the past four years, and that he be requested to accept the office for the ensuing year.—This resolution was carried unanimously, and the President on taking the chair briefly returned thanks.

ANNUAL MEETING,
May 1st, 1884.
Major Allen, President, in the chair.

The Committee were again able to report most thankfully that the Hospital has maintained its character for usefulness and efficiency during the past year. The pressure of applications has been very great, as many as a hundred persons sometimes waiting for admission. The number of applications for admission from May 1st, 1883, to April 30th, 1884, were 1340. That for the preceding year was 1280. 984

patients have been admitted, and 784 have been discharged, leaving 143 in the Hospital at the present date. The Donations amounted to £724 6s. 11d., including—Earl of Portsmouth, £21; Thomas Scott, Esq., £52; a Friend, per E. Skeate, Esq., £100; R. Formby, Esq., £100; E. H. Wiggett, Esq., £40; Montagu Williams, Esq., £100; Great Western Railway Company, £20. The Collections at churches in Bath increased from £68 13s. 3d. last year to £106 12s. 9d. The thanks of the Committee are gratefully tendered to those clergymen who have allowed sermons to be preached and collections made in their churches, and also to the clergymen who have preached the sermons. At churches in the country the collections amounted to £114 14s. 9d. During the year the amount received from Legacies has been unusually large, including £1000 from the late Wm. Smith, Esq., and the balance of the long-pending reversionary bequest of the late Mr. Thomas Blann. The following amounts have also been received:— Miss Holburn, £100; Mrs. Bush, £100; Miss F. Vicary, £19 19s.

During the year a change has taken place in the staff of the Hospital. Mr. Alexander R. Busby, in consequence of ill-health, tendered his resignation as Resident Medical Officer, and in accepting it with great regret at losing his services, the best thanks of the Committee were voted to him for the faithful, zealous, and highly satisfactory manner in which he had discharged the duties during the two years he had held the appointment. The vacancy was filled up by the election of Mr. James Merces, who came into residence in January last. Miss Brooke, who has been matron at the Hospital for nearly 32 years, has also through failing health resigned, and the Committee desire to record their appreciation of her valuable services during such a long period of years. Miss Hellings, of St. Mary's Hospital, Paddington, was elected in her stead.

There are five vacancies in the list of elected Governors, caused by the resignation of Sir Henry Freeling, Bart., and General Wylde, and by the decease of the following gentlemen: J. Todd, Esq., Dr. Thos. Sandon Watson (who was elected in 1835, and was one of the physicians to the Hospital for 33 years), and of F. B. Gill, Esq., who until failing health was an active member of the Committee.

The Committee have also to record the loss the Institution has sustained by the deaths of Sir E. B. Baker, Bart., Miss Birch, G. D. Wingfield Digby, Esq. (in 1875 President of the Hospital), and Sir A. H. Elton, Bart., who became Governors by virtue of their benefactions to the Hospital.

The General Committee, Sub-Committee, and Treasurers were appointed for the ensuing year.

Major Allen, after returning thanks to the Governors and Officials for the assistance rendered him during the five years he has been President, retired from the chair, which was taken by Mr. Murch, senior Vice-President, who, after speaking of the admirable manner in which the duties had been carried out by Major Allen, proposed that Lord Brooke, M.P., be elected President for the ensuing year.—This was seconded by Mr. R. S. Blaine, and carried unanimously.

Lord Brooke, having taken the chair, returned thanks for the honour conferred upon him.

The Mayor of Bath, in eulogistic terms, proposed,— That at this Court the Governors desire to present their best thanks to Major Ralph S. Allen for the faithful and zealous discharge of the duties of President, and for the care and attention he has shown to the interests of the Hospital during the five years he has held the office; and would wish to express to him the deep sense which they entertain of his valuable services.—This was seconded by Mr. John Stone, and carried by acclamation.—Major Allen briefly replied.

ANNUAL MEETING,
May 1st, 1885.

Major Allen, Senior Vice-President, in the chair.

The number of applications for admission has been 1420. At present 133 patients are awaiting admission. The daily average in the Hospital has been 128, and the average duration of residence 45¾ days. Although the institution, by death and other circumstances, lost some of its supporters, the Committee have pleasure in stating that the Annual Subscriptions have not diminished. The collections in Churches and Chapels in Bath, amounting to £77 12s. 7d., are rather less than last year, but the contributions from Country Parishes, amounting to £147 6s., have increased by £35 11s. 3d. The donations, £468 14s. 6d., though less than last year, are above the average. The following legacies have been received :—Dr. T. Sandon Watson, £100; Mrs. M. Chappell, £20; Miss S. A. Beak, ¼ of Residue, £404 4s. 6d. The Hospital expenses for repairs have been heavier than usual, owing to the painting of the two large Day Wards and of the lower part of the walls of the Night Wards. Mr. C. T. Griffiths has been elected as Resident Medical Officer, *vice* Mr. J. Merces resigned. During the past year this Institution, in common with other Local Charities, has sustained a loss by the death of Major T. R. Baker, who was elected a Governor in 1853, and served the office of President in 1864. He was also, until lately, an active member of the Committee. Capt. Bradshaw, who was a liberal contributor to the funds of the Hospital, and formerly a member of the Committee, has also died. There are, therefore, two vacancies in the list of Elected Governors to be filled up.—After some discussion on the manner of electing the Committee, the General Committee, Sub-Committee, and Treasurers were appointed for the ensuing year. Major Allen, having vacated the chair, it was taken by Mr. Burningham.

Col. Cockell proposed—That the best thanks of the Governors be presented to Major Allen, for the efficient manner in which, as Senior Vice-President, he has performed the duties of Chairman during the past year, in the unavoidable absence of the President, Lord Brooke, and that he be requested to undertake the Office of President for the ensuing year. Mr. Blaine seconded, and the resolution was unanimously carried.

ANNUAL MEETING,
May 1st, 1886.
Major Allen in the chair.

During the year just closed, 1426 applications have been received, 1063 patients have been admitted, making, with 134 patients remaining in the house at commencement of year, a total of 1197; of these 1056 have been discharged and 141 are in the Hospital. Of those discharged 130 were cured, 868 greatly benefited, 23 no better, 17 unfit, 6 discharged at their own request, 9 for misconduct, and 3 have died. Daily average in Hospital had been 133, and the average duration of residence 46 days. Annual subscriptions amounted to £1,327 4s. 6d., being a slight increase. The donations were £407 4s. 5d., which was £61 10s. 1d. less than last year. The following legacies have been received: Miss Birch (and interest), £31 6s.; Miss Dobson (less duty), £90; Miss Domager, £200.

With reference to the remarks made by the President at the Quarterly Court in October last respecting the large number of persons waiting for vacancies, a Sub-Committee was appointed to consider what means, if any, could be devised to reduce the constant pressure, and after holding several meetings and thoroughly discussing the matter, made a Report which was unanimously adopted by your Committee.

That Report recommended that in the Wards, originally built for infectious cases, the partitions should be removed and other minor alterations effected, by which ten extra Beds would be obtained for Male Patients. Five additional Beds for Females would be placed in the existing Wards; this increased accommodation of fifteen Beds being as large as present circumstances admitted.

Amongst the Governors whom the Hospital has lost by death during the year, there is one especially deserving honourable mention. Mr. William Long had filled the office for 42 years, devoting to it in the earlier part of this long period much time and attention. During three successive years, 1857-58-59, he occupied the chair of President, having twice been re-elected in consequence of his valuable aid in all the discussions as to an enlargement of the Hospital.

The ceremony of laying the foundation stone of the new building took place during the third year of his Presidency; and Dr. Falconer being Mayor, in his speech on the occasion, paid a just tribute to the zeal, energy, and ability with which the President had promoted the undertaking. Mr. Long had been for many years one of the Vice-Presidents of the Hospital, and though, in consequence of removal from Bath and long continued ill-health, he had been unable to attend the meetings, he retained a warm interest in its welfare, and his name will always be gratefully and affectionately remembered.

In addition to Mr. Long, the deceased Governors are Captain Sainsbury, the Rev. C. R. Davy, and the Rev. A. G. How, making four vacancies to be filled up.

Mr. Benjamin Starr, who resigned the appointment of Registrar in 1880, after holding the office for 40 years, has also died during the past year.

The Committee gratefully acknowledge the contributions given during the past two or three years by some of the Livery Companies of London, viz., the "Skinners," "Grocers," "Armourers and Braziers," "Mercers' Company," and "Trustees of Prison Charities."

Moved by Mr. Murch, seconded by Mr. H. D. Skrine, and resolved :—That this meeting wishes to record its deep sense of the loss by death of four Governors of the Hospital during the past year—the Rev. C. R. Davy, Captain Sainsbury, the Rev. A. G. How, and Mr. William Long, all much respected. It cannot be forgotten that Mr. Long filled the office of President three successive years, in which he gave unremitting attention to the erection of the new wing, in addition to his generous pecuniary contribution. As Governor for the long period of 42 years, and Vice-President nearly 31, he always took a warm interest in the welfare of the institution, and for this and other eminent services to the city of Bath his memory deserves to be long and gratefully remembered. That a copy of this resolution be sent to Colonel Long, assuring him that the Governors desire to express their deepest sympathy with the family in their bereavement.

Major Allen having thanked the Governors for the kind support afforded him during his Presidency, vacated the Chair, which was taken by Mr. Jerom Murch, Senior Vice-President, who moved :—That the very constant attendance and other eminent services of Major Allen during six years in which he has been President of the Hospital, demand the grateful acknowledgment of the Governors; that they regret his retirement sincerely, but hope still to have the benefit of his valuable co-operation.

This was seconded by His Honour, Judge Caillard, and carried by acclamation.

Major Allen having briefly replied, Mr. Murch proposed that General Jervois be elected President for the ensuing year, which being seconded, was unanimously agreed to.

General Jervois having taken the Chair, thanked the Governors for the honour conferred upon him.

ANNUAL MEETING.

May 2nd, 1887.
General Jervois, President, in the chair.

In making their Annual Report to the Governors,

the Committee of the Bath Mineral Water Hospital are glad to be able to state that during the year ending 30th April, 1887, the Hospital has fully maintained its character for usefulness and efficiency.

The increased accommodation of 15 beds referred to in the last Annual Report, has been a great boon, but in consequence of the patients having remained longer, the total number passed through the Hospital is less than was anticipated.

On the 1st of May, 1886, 141 patients were in the House, and during the year just closed, 1,433 applications for admission have been made, from the number of which 1,115 Patients have been admitted, making the total number in the Hospital 1,256. Of these 1,096 have been discharged, leaving in the Hospital this day 160.

Of those discharged 137 were cured, 900 were greatly benefited, 33 no better, 12 partially, 4 were discharged at their own request, 6 for misbehaviour, and 4 have died.

The daily average in the Hospital has been 146, and the average duration of residence $48\frac{1}{2}$ days. Last year the daily average was 133, and average stay 46 days. Nearly 100 persons are now waiting for vacancies.

The gratitude constantly expressed by patients on their discharge convinces the Committee that the benefits of the Charity are highly appreciated.

The financial position of all institutions dependent to a great extent upon the support of the public for their maintenance, must necessarily be a source of some anxiety to their Managers, but the Committee have pleasure in reporting that notwithstanding the much regretted loss of several old subscribers, and the continued Agricultural and Commercial depression, the Annual Subscriptions have slightly increased, amounting this year to £1,341 6s. 6d.

The Donations (including the handsome sum of £500 given by G. Stuckey Lean, Esq., "In Memoriam") have amounted to £946 15s. 3d.

Application has again been made to the London Livery Companies, and the following contributions received :—The Worshipful Company of Saddlers, £5 5s.; The Trustees of Prison Charities (3rd donation), £10 10s.

In September last a large number of the Colonial and Indian Commissioners visited the Hospital, with which they were greatly pleased.

Prominent among the losses experienced during the past year, has been that caused by the sudden death of Major Ralph Shuttleworth Allen, which occasions a vacancy in the list of elected Governors. With reference to this sad event, the following resolution was entered on the minutes :—

"That the Committee desire to record their feeling of deep sorrow at the loss which this Hospital (in common with other Institutions in the City of Bath) has sustained by the sudden death of their late President, Major Ralph Shuttleworth Allen, who by his kindness and courtesy, gained the respect and esteem of those who enjoyed the privilege of his friendship.

"He was elected a Governor in 1862, and since 1864 has been annually elected a Member of the Committee. In 1873 he was appointed President, the office of which he also served during the years 1879 to 1883 inclusive, and again during the year 1885-6, a greater number of times than any previous President.

He was most regular in his attendance and took the greatest interest in the welfare of the Institution, with which his family has been associated from its foundation; and his firm judgment and tact enabled him to overcome many difficulties which arose.

"It was his suggestion, during the last year of his Presidency, which led to the increased accommodation which has been provided for 15 additional Patients.

"At the time of his decease he was a Vice-President and one of the Treasurers, and as recently as the Thursday before his death, was present at the weekly meeting of the Committee."

It may be interesting to note that this year the Hospital celebrates its 3rd Jubilee, the movement which led to its establishment having been commenced in 1737, and shortly afterwards the Plans were submitted to His Majesty King George II., and the Royal Family.

The Minutes of the last General Court and subsequent proceedings of the Committee were read and confirmed. The foregoing Report of the Committee and the Financial Statement of the year read. The usual routine business was then gone through, and the ordinary Resolution regarding the Report was adopted.

General Jervois having thanked the Governors for the kind support received from them during the year, vacated the chair, which was taken by His Worship the Mayor of Bath (Mr. Jerom Murch, Senior Vice-President).

It was moved by Mr. Burningham, seconded by Mr. Hammond:—"That the best thanks of the Governors be awarded to General Jervois for his past valuable services as President of the Hospital, and that he be requested to assume that office for the coming year.

The Resolution was carried unanimously, and the President on taking the chair, briefly returned thanks.

Since the Annual Meeting a letter has been received from the Secretary of State, Home Department, Whitehall, London, stating that "Her Majesty has been graciously pleased to command that this Hospital shall be called 'The Royal Mineral Water Hospital, Bath,'" to which reference is further made on pages 146 and 147.

ANNUAL MEETING.
May 1st, 1888.

General Jervois, President, in the Chair.

The Committee are most thankful to be again able to report that the Hospital has maintained its character for usefulness and efficiency during the past year. The number of applications for admisson has been 1405. The previous year the number was 1433. 1070 patients have been admitted, making the total number (including those in the house on the 1st of May last) 1230. 1070 patients have been discharged, leaving in the Hospital this day 160. Of those discharged, 122 were cured; 897 were greatly benefited; 25 were no better; 10 were unfit; 8 were discharged at their own request; 5 were discharged for misbehaviour, and 3 have died. The daily average in the house has been 145, and the average stay of each patient 49½ days. Upwards of 100 persons are now waiting for vacancies.

The Annual Subscriptions from private persons have amounted to £597 1s. 6d., and from Poor Law Unions and Parishes to £777 18s. The Donations, amounting to £297 10s. 5d., are about £650 less than last year. The following Legacies have been received: Miss H. M. Coney, £48; Mr. W. Lucas, £90; Mr. C. J. Thornley, £45.

The thanks of the Committee are hereby given to the clergymen who have allowed Collections to be made in their churches on behalf of the Hospital, and also to the clergymen who have preached the sermons.

The Collections at churches in Bath have amounted to £92 2s. 2d., being £12 10s. 4d. more than last year. At churches in the country the Collections realised £116 6s. 3d., being £14 5s. 9d. less than last year.

The expenditure of the Hospital during the year, including the cost of fitting up the new blanket and drying room, is about £190 less than in the previous year.

Assent has been given, so far as the interests of this Institution are involved, to the scheme of the Chancellor of the Exchequer for the conversion of the Three per Cent. Stocks. This will entail a loss of income to the extent of £66 15s. 0d. per annum until 1903, and of £133 10s. 0d. afterwards, unless the investments are altered in the meantime.

Shortly after the last Annual Meeting a letter was received from the Secretary of State for the Home Department, stating that Her Majesty had been pleased to command that this Hospital shall henceforth be called the " Royal Mineral Water Hospital." The Committee consider that a great honour has been

Chapter IV.

conferred on this national charity, which since its foundation has received donations from the following members of the Royal Family, viz.:—

In	1737,	His Majesty King George II. ...	£200
,,	,,	H.R.H. The Prince of Wales	300
,,	,,	H.R.H. The Princess of Wales ...	100
,,	,,	H.R.H. The Princess Amelia ...	100
,,	1746,	H.R.H. The Princess Caroline ..	100
,,	1752,	H.R.H. The Duke of Cumberland	100
,,	,,	H.R.H. The Princess Amelia ...	100
,,	1761,	H.R.H. The Duke of York	50
,,	1796,	H.R.H. The Prince of Wales ...	105
,,	1817,	H.R.H. The Princess Elizabeth	50
,,	1859,	H.R.H. The Prince of Wales ..	100

Special thanks are given to Col. Laurie, C.B., one of the members for Bath, for his kind assistance in the matter, as well as for the contribution given by the Saddlers' Company, of which he is the Master.

The Royal Arms, carved in Portland stone, have been placed on the pediment of the Hospital facing Milsom Street.

On the occasion of Her Majesty's Jubilee, the Hospital was illuminated, and the patients provided with a dinner suitable to the occasion. A musical entertainment was also given during the day.

As mentioned in previous reports, a large number of the poor are sent from many populous and wealthy Unions and parishes, and especially from London, but in some cases the Boards of Guardians decline to make the pecuniary contributions in aid of the funds which the Act of Parliament allows, and which are required for the support of the Hospital. If the poor rates of such Unions and parishes are lightened by the maintenance of their cripples, and if by the timely cure or alleviation of ailments future pauperism is prevented, it seems only just that this Institution should receive some pecuniary acknowledgment.

The Committee regret the loss by death during the year of several very useful and esteemed Governors, viz. :—The Rev. Thomas Woodward, elected in 1851, but who had left Bath many years ; also Capt. Breton, R.N., elected in 1859, and who, until his health failed, was an active member of the Committee, and one of the Vice-Presidents. The loss of Major Manley, who was elected in 1879, will also be greatly felt. He was a very regular attendant at the weekly meetings of the Committee, and was most useful in the House Sub-Committee. The Rev. T. P. Rogers, who was elected at the last Annual Meeting, died suddenly a short time since. Robt. Cook, Esq., who became a Governor in 1845 by virtue of his donation, has also died. The vacancies caused by the four first-named will have to be filled up at the Annual Meeting.

In conclusion, the Committee confidently entertain the hope that an Institution, which extensively relieves the sufferings of humanity, and enables many of the working classes to recover the means of maintaining their families, will continue to receive the support it so well deserves.

The Minutes of the last General Court and the subsequent proceedings of the Committee, were read and confirmed.

The foregoing report of the Committee, and the financial statement of the year, were read.

Mr. A. P. Falconer moved, Dr. Cardew seconded, and it was resolved,—That the report, together with the accounts for the year, be received and adopted, and that copies thereof be printed and sent to every Governor, Subscriber, and Donor, as well as the

Chapter IV.

officiating clergy and Nonconformist ministers in Bath and its vicinity.

The Committe, Sub-Committees, and Treasurers were appointed for the coming year.

General Jervois, having thanked the Governors for the kind support received from them during the two years he had been President, vacated the chair, which was taken by Mr. Burningham, Vice-President, who moved that General Mainwaring be elected President of the Hospital for the ensuing year.

This was seconded by Colonel Vaughton, and carried unanimously. The President, on taking the chair, briefly returned thanks.

A vote of thanks to the retiring President was carried by acclamation, on the proposition of Mr. J. T. Rainey, seconded by Colonel Fanshawe.

STATEMENT OF PATIENTS ADMITTED AND DISCHARGED.

Remaining in the House, April 30, 1887	160	
Admitted from May 1, 1887, to April 30, 1888	1070	
		1230
Discharged from May 1, 1887, to May 1, 1888	1070	
Remaining in the House	160	
		1230

The daily average number in the House, 145; average stay, 49½ days.

PATIENTS DISCHARGED FROM MAY, 1742, TO MAY, 1888.

Recovered	16,151
Relieved	34,506
No better	4,172
Unfit	4,772

At their own desire or for Misbehaviour ...	853
Died	762
Total	**61,216**

As I think it would be impossible to describe more eloquently and appropriately the great blessings which are placed within the reach of the suffering poor of the United Kingdom, through the instrumentality of the "Royal Mineral Water Hospital, Bath," I shall in conclusion, repeat Dr. R. W. Falconer's remarks, at the end of his edition. The hand which wrote them is still, but the words are as applicable now as when they were written nearly 25 years ago. In fact, owing to improvements of various kinds which have been carried out during that period, patients now admitted to the Hospital are placed under conditions more favourable to rapid and complete recovery than when Dr. Falconer wrote.

The durable effects of these improvements are made manifest in two ways—First, in the shortened period of detention necessary in the Hospital; and, secondly, in the greater number of patients which are treated annually in the Institution.

It is to be earnestly hoped that the time may never arrive when funds, sufficient, to meet the necessary expenditure of this noble Institution, should be found wanting, and that nothing may occur to oblige the Governors to draw on capital, or to decrease the number of admissions. It will be seen that the numbers of applicants for admission are increasing year by year, and it is to be hoped that a generous public will nobly support this Institution and enable it to continue to diffuse its widely-extended benefits in the future, as it has done during the past 146 years.

"Few charities have numbered among their warm supporters so many eminent persons as the Bath General Hospital. The enumeration of some, only out of many, who have held the office of President of the Corporation will indicate the estimation in which it was held. In the list of Presidents, we find the following:—H.R.H. the Prince of Wales; H.R.H. the Duke of York; the Archbishop of Canterbury (Dr. Secker); the Earl of Northington (Lord High Chancellor of England); the Dukes of Beaufort, Bedford, Devonshire, Marlborough, Montague, Kingston, Leeds, and Northumberland; the Marquises of Rockingham, Stafford, Carnarvon, Bath, and Thomond; the Earls of Chesterfield, Lincoln, Kerry, Guildford, Spencer, Ailesbury, Camden, Mansfield, Nugent, Manvers, Bridgewater, Brecknock, Liverpool, and Pembroke; besides many Commoners of distinction.

"Of the benefits which the Bath General Hospital has directly conferred upon the sick and suffering poor of Great Britain and Ireland, and indirectly upon the parishes in former times, and upon the Unions at the present time, some idea may be formed, when it is stated, that between May, 1742, and May, 1863, 41,227 patients have been admitted into the Hospital, of which number, 12,142 have been recovered, and 20,446 have been relieved by its means.*

"It should be remembered that the benefits of this charity are not confined to its immediate locality, but are freely open to the whole Kingdom; that the act of its incorporation constituted it a National Charity, and provided for the admission of all cases from the United Kingdom of poor persons suffering from sick-

* The total number of patients discharged between 1742 and May 1st, 1888, was 61,216.

ness which may be relieved by the Bath Mineral Waters, without the necessity of any other recommendation or interest being exercised on their behalf.

"As a National Charity, as a charity which has during its existence been the means of relieving a vast amount of suffering, it commends itself to the benevolent and charitable of the United Kingdom, and may therefore expect from them that aid and assistance, which is always required to meet the expenditure necessary for the full and satisfactory management of a large and important Hospital."

A. BEAUFORT BRABAZON, M.D.

www.ingramcontent.com/pod-product-compliance
Lightning Source LLC
Chambersburg PA
CBHW030341170426
43202CB00010B/1205